GW00467497

Business
BENCHMARK

Pre-Intermediate to Intermediate
Preliminary

Personal Study Book

Norman Whitby

CAMBRIDGE
UNIVERSITY PRESS

CAMBRIDGE UNIVERSITY PRESS
Cambridge, New York, Melbourne, Madrid, Cape Town,
Singapore, São Paulo, Delhi, Tokyo, Mexico City

Cambridge University Press
The Edinburgh Building, Cambridge CB2 8RU, UK

www.cambridge.org
Information on this title: www.cambridge.org/9780521672863

First published 2006
8th printing 2011

Printed in the United Kingdom at the University Press, Cambridge

A catalogue record for this publication is available from the British Library

ISBN 978-0-521-67286-3 Personal Study Book Pre-Intermediate to Intermediate/Preliminary
ISBN 978-0-521-67117-0 Student's Book BEC Preliminary Edition
ISBN 978-0-521-67284-9 Student's Book BULATS Edition Pre-Intermediate to Intermediate with CD-ROM
ISBN 978-0-521-67285-6 Teacher's Resource Book Pre-Intermediate to Intermediate/Preliminary
ISBN 978-0-521-67287-0 Audio Cassette BEC Preliminary Edition
ISBN 978-0-521-67288-7 Audio CD BEC Preliminary Edition
ISBN 978-0-521-67657-1 Audio Cassette BULATS Edition Pre-Intermediate to Intermediate
ISBN 978-0-521-67658-8 Audio CD BULATS Edition Pre-Intermediate to Intermediate

Author's note

To the student

This Personal Study Book provides you with two pages of extra exercises and activities for each unit of the Student's Book. The exercises and activities are designed to reinforce what you have studied and they cover vocabulary, grammar, reading and writing.

It is a good idea to do the work in each unit of the Personal Study Book *after* you have finished the unit in the Student's Book. This will help you to remember things you have studied. You will need to write your answers in your notebook. Do the exercises regularly while the things you have studied in the Student's Book are still fresh in your memory.

Check your answers by looking in the key on pages 70–78. If you are not sure why an answer in the key is correct, ask your teacher to explain.

When you do the writing exercises, you can compare your answer with a sample answer in the answer key. If your teacher agrees, you can give him/her your answer to correct.

If you are preparing for the Cambridge ESOL BEC Preliminary exam or the BULATS Test, a number of exercises are designed to develop your exam skills.

The Personal Study Book also contains a Word list. These are words and phrases from the units and recording transcripts of the Student's Book which may be unfamiliar to you, or difficult to understand. When you find new words in the Student's Book, always try to guess the meaning first from the context. Keep a list of new vocabulary in your notebook. In general, use the Word list to check the meanings later, not while you are doing the exercises in the Student's Book.

Acknowledgements

The author and publishers are grateful to the following for permission to produce copyright material. It has not always been possible to identify the sources of all the material used and in such cases the publishers would welcome information from the copyright owners.

p.12: Diana Cambridge for adapted article 'Foibles, Signoffs', *The Guardian*, 14 June 2004. Used by permission of Diana Cambridge; p.31: Crown Publishers for the adapted text on p.127 from *Talking with Confidence for the Painfully Shy*. Copyright © 1997 Don Gabor. Used by permission of Crown Publishers, a division of Random House, Inc; p.38: *The Economist* for graph 'Indonesia's employment rate'. © The Economist Newspaper Limited, London, 25 September 2004; p.40 Barry Scanes for his help with this exercise; p.44: Hasbro Inc. (http://www.hasbro.com) for adapted article 'Parker Brothers Company History'. © 2005 Hasbro Inc. Used with permission.

Illustrations on pages 14 and 38 by Tim Oliver.

Contents

UNIT 1 The working day

Vocabulary

Many students record the words that they want to learn by writing them in a list with a translation next to each one. This is not usually the best way of doing it because:

- the words are not organised into topics
- it does not tell you how to use the words.

Words are often easier to remember if you put them into groups based on the meaning.

1 Write the words from the box next to the most suitable company department to make three word diagrams.

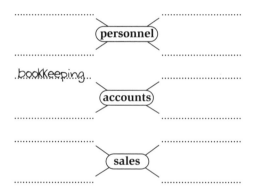

~~bookkeeping~~
consumer
expenditure
human resources
mail order
payroll
recruitment
retail outlet
salary
staff
wholesale
workforce

2 Can you add any more words to the diagrams? Use your dictionary if you like.

Another way to group words is to take one word and record other words that can be formed from it by adding prefixes and suffixes.

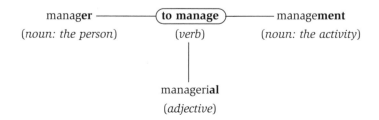

3 Write the correct word from the box next to the correct definition in the word diagram below.

1 ....
the thing that a company produces

2 ....
the company or person who produces something

3 ....
the action of producing something, or the quantity produced

4 ....
a measure which compares the value of what a company produces with the time and money it spends

(to produce)

> producer
> product
> production
> productivity

4 Now use your dictionary to make a similar diagram around the verb *to employ*.

Grammar

Read the article and then write the questions for the answers (1–6) in your notebook.

AUDIENCE NUMBERS DOWN FOR RADIO HEARTBEAT

Things are not looking good at Radio Heartbeat at the moment. Their new breakfast show presenter, Johnny Race, just can't keep the listeners. He only attracts 30,000 listeners each morning whereas 45,000 people regularly listen to the rival station, Hugz. Even more worrying for Heartbeat is the success of Marie Riley's new breakfast show over on Shire Radio. According to opinion surveys, people especially like the interviews on her show.

Heartbeat's chief executive, David Webb, says that he is not worried by the figures. 'We're trying to appeal to younger listeners now,' he says. 'They need time to find us. Johnny's got a great personality and I'm sure he can bring them in. We have every confidence in him.'

Unfortunately, now Heartbeat's teatime DJ, Morgan Wells, says he is thinking of leaving the station. If he does, this will be another major blow for Radio Heartbeat.

---

1 How many listeners does Johnny Race attract?
   30 thousand each day.
2 The interviews.
3 No, he isn't worried.
4 Younger listeners.
5 Because has a great personality.
6 Leaving Radio Heartbeat.

2 Corporate culture

Reading

Read the following culture statement from a bank and decide which paragraph is about the following. Write the correct paragraph number in each box.

- staff development   ⬛3⬛
- after-work activities   ☐
- working hours   ☐
- equal opportunities   ☐

COMMUNITY BANK CALIFORNIA   Our Culture

1   We offer a lively working culture in which we're confident you'll feel at home. In return, we'll expect you to work hard and take responsibility for what you do.

2   As an organisation, we recognise the benefits of attracting staff from a wide range of backgrounds. We carry out regular diversity training and monitoring. In addition, we have recently commissioned reports on disability access and race equality in the workplace.

3   Our strong commitment to training reflects a learning culture which encourages movement across departments and progression within the Bank. We provide regular assessments so that you'll always be aware of your performance. We can also provide support to study for professional qualifications.

4   The Bank also recognises the value of flexible working. We encourage a work–life balance by allowing flexible working arrangements. You can balance periods of intensive work by coming in a little later or leaving a little earlier at other times. This allows you to enjoy a good social life and can help with your family commitments.

5   If you are a keen sportsperson, you can play a variety of sports at the Bank, socially or competitively. Many of our bank teams travel to other central banks to compete. In addition we are hoping to open our new Head Office gym by the end of next year. We also have discounted rates for trips to the theatre.

Vocabulary

Collocations are words which are often used together (see page 15 in the Student's Book).

1 In your notebook, write four verb–noun collocations and four adjective–noun collocations from the Community Bank text that you think are useful to remember.

2 Match the following words (1–4) with the correct definition (a–d).

1 a loan   2 a mortgage   3 interest   4 an overdraft

a An agreement with the bank which allows you to spend more money than you have in your account.
b A sum of money which you borrow from a bank or person for a period of time.
c A sum of extra money which you pay when you pay back a sum that you borrowed.
d A sum of money which you borrow from the bank so that you can buy a house.

3 Match the words in column A with those in column B to make compound nouns connected with banking. You can use some words twice.

A	B
credit	account
current	rate
deposit	debit
standing	card
overdraft	facility
direct	order
cash	point
interest	dispenser
mortgage	

4 Complete these definitions with the correct compound nouns.

1 A/an _current account_ is a bank account for writing cheques and paying bills.
2 A/an .... is a bank account for saving money for a long time.
3 The .... is the interest that the bank charges on a loan, expressed as a percentage.
4 A .... is an instruction to a bank to make a regular payment to someone.
5 A .... is an agreement that a company can regularly collect an amount of money from their customer's bank account (for example to pay bills).

Grammar

1 **Read the following text to find out about the history of Wipro Technologies.**

WIPRO TECHNOLOGIES

Wipro is one of India's biggest software and electronics companies. Its customer list includes Sony, Microsoft and Nokia and it generally makes a yearly profit of over $200 million. But Wipro is also an example of a company which began as something very different from what it is now.

Mr M.H. Premji originally founded the company in the 1940s. At that time it was called Western India Vegetable Products Ltd and it manufactured vegetable oil and soap. Mr Premji's son, Azim Premji, went to Stanford University in California to study engineering but he did not finish his studies. In 1966, following the death of his father, he returned to India and took over the business. Under Azim Premji, the company began a programme of expansion and started to produce a number of other completely different products. These included lights and baby care products.

In the 1970s and 1980s, the government's economic policies stopped many multinational companies from trading in India. Global IT companies like IBM left the country and Wipro moved into this field. Azim Premji set up the first IT business in Bangalore in 1980 and the company soon expanded into other IT areas such as system design. In the 1990s, the government reopened the markets and many multinational companies returned to India. At the same time, Wipro began working on product engineering for customers in the USA and also launched a global IT services division.

In 2001, the magazine *Business Today* named Wipro India's most valuable company and Azim Premji is now one of the richest men in the country.

---

2 **Put the verb in brackets in the sentences (1–6) below into the past simple form, either affirmative or negative, to make true sentences about Wipro.**

1 Mr M.H. Premji, the founder, did not call the company Wipro Technologies. (call)

2 Mr M.H. Premji .... the company in the 1940s and 1950s. (run)

3 In the 1940s, the company .... baby care products. (make)

4 In the 1970s and 1980s, the government .... the activity of multinational companies in India. (limit)

5 During the 1980s, IBM .... in India. (operate)

6 In the 1980s, Wipro .... customers in the USA. (have)

3 Now write questions for the following answers.

1 When did Mr. M.H. Premji found the company?
In the 1940s.
2 Vegetable oil and soap.
3 Stanford University in California.
4 In 1966.
5 Because of the government's economic policies.
6 In 1980.

Writing

1 Rachel Elnaugh started a company called 'Red Letter Days'. The company provides special, once-in-a-lifetime experiences, such as flying a plane, which you can give to people as presents. Read these notes about Rachel Elnaugh.

1965: born in Chelmsford, UK

1983: left school, went to work in accountant's office

1985: moved to London, worked as tax consultant

1989: had idea for company 'Red Letter Days'. (Idea came from trying to find a special birthday present for her father.)

1991: started advertising in national newspapers

2000: opened branch in Scotland

2004: opened third office

2005: AIC, an investment consultancy, took over the management of the company

2 You work for 'Red Letter Days' and need to write a short profile of the company's founder to put on the company website. Using the notes above, write the profile. Remember to put in any small words which are missing like pronouns and articles.

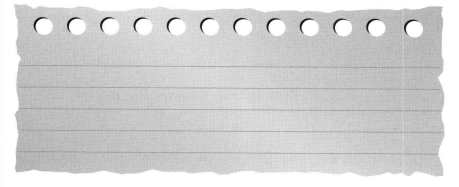

4 The Internet

Writing

1 Read the following article which gives advice about writing emails. Is there anything that you write in emails that it does not recommend?

HOW DO I SAY IT ON EMAIL?

Sometimes it takes me a long time to decide what I should write at the end of an email. Yours what? Yours sincerely, yours truly, yours faithfully? Kind regards, best regards, best wishes or regards? Love and kisses if you have a close relationship? 'Kind regards' seems to be the most usual sign-off in business. It is best to put something, because emails without a sign-off can look unfriendly.

You should avoid funny phrases like 'keep smiling'. Never try to show how busy your life is by finishing with 'yours in haste' or using abbreviations like 'yrs' or 'regs'. In fact, it is best not to use abbreviations like 'asap' at all unless they are usual in your line of business. Spellings like 'thanx' instead of 'thanks' or '4u' instead of 'for you' are not acceptable in business emails.

Underlining words or PUTTING THINGS IN CAPITALS is the written equivalent of shouting at someone. It can make you seem childish or emotional. Using a lot of exclamation marks (!!!!) and emoticons like ☺ can have the same effect.

Adapted from *The Guardian*

2 Read the following email. The writer does not follow the advice in the article. Underline the words and expressions which should be changed.

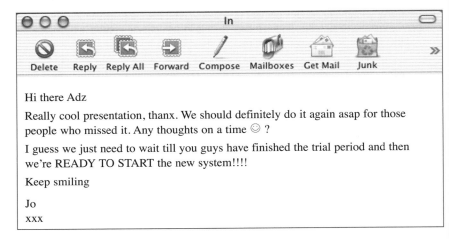

Hi there Adz

Really cool presentation, thanx. We should definitely do it again asap for those people who missed it. Any thoughts on a time ☺ ?

I guess we just need to wait till you guys have finished the trial period and then we're READY TO START the new system!!!!

Keep smiling

Jo

xxx

3 Rewrite the email from Exercise 2 in your notebook, so that it follows the advice in the article. Keep the tone friendly, but change any language you think is too informal.

Vocabulary

1 Match the words (1–9) with the correct definitions (a–i).

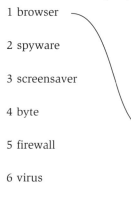

1 browser

2 spyware

3 screensaver

4 byte

5 firewall

6 virus

7 hacker

8 spam

9 server

a   A programme which secretly monitors your actions on the computer.

b   A computer on a network which carries out all the functions for a particular purpose, e.g. email.

c   Emails which have not been asked for (usually advertising). They are also called *junk mail*.

d   Software which is used to find and display webpages.

e   Someone who enters a computer system without permission.

f   A unit of storage on a computer (which can hold one character).

g   The picture on a computer screen when you are not using it.

h   A programme that enters your computer and makes copies of itself. It can destroy the information on your computer.

i   A programme which checks the information coming from the Internet onto your computer.

2 Circle the correct word in each of these sentences (1–6).

1   I tried to send the document by email but it came back to me with a message to say that it was too big to go through the *screensaver/firewall/spam*.

2   My friend sent me a warning today about a new *virus/server/firewall* which can damage the files on your hard drive.

3   Are you tired of looking at the same *hacker/browser/screensaver*? Browse our collection of pictures and download your favourite today!

4   There is a possibility that *browsers/hackers/bytes* have gained access to confidential information on the computer.

5   Our filter will stop over 90 per cent of *spam/spyware/bytes* from entering your inbox. Download the 30-day free trial now!

6   I'm afraid you can't check your email at the moment. The *hacker/screensaver/server* is down.

5 Describing equipment

Vocabulary

> You can describe the shape of an object with a noun or a verb:
>
> *It's a rectangle.*   (noun)
> *It's rectangular.*   (adjective)

1 Complete the table with the correct nouns and adjectives. Sometimes they are the same word. Use a dictionary to help you if necessary.

Noun	Adjective
a circle	
an oval	
	triangular
	square
a sphere	
	cylindrical
a cone	

> Other shapes can be described by comparing them with something, like letters of the alphabet:
>
>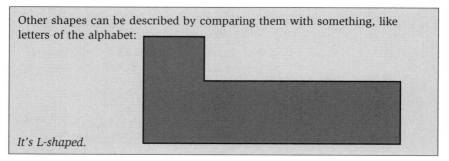
>
> *It's L-shaped.*

2 How could you describe the following shapes?

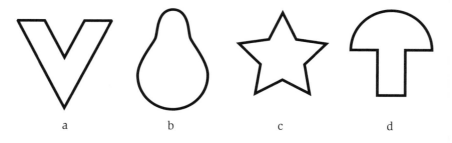

a   b   c   d

3 Match the raw materials (1–8) with each company's products (a–h).

1 aluminium ——— a luxury items of clothing, mainly ties and shirts
2 silk ———b cans for drinks
3 cellophane   c designer bags and other smaller items such as wallets
4 glass   d designer knitwear
5 cotton   e optical fibre for telecommunications
6 leather   f clothing including socks, shirts and sportswear
7 wool   g packaging for mass-produced goods, e.g. T-shirts
8 steel   h kitchen equipment such as knives and saucepans

4 Think of a company and write down the English names of the raw materials that it uses. Use a dictionary if necessary.

5 There is a group of phrasal verbs that we often use to talk about using electrical equipment. Circle the correct answer for each question.

1 What should you do if you can't hear the TV very well?
A Turn it up **B** Turn it down

2 What should you do if the TV is too loud?
A Turn it down **B** Turn it on

3 What should you do if you don't want your mobile phone to ring?
A Switch it on **B** Switch it off

4 What should you do if you need to recharge your phone battery?
A Turn it on **B** Plug it into the mains

5 What should you do when your phone battery is fully charged again?
A Plug it into the mains **B** Unplug it

6 What should you do if the heater is working but the room is cold?
A Turn it up **B** Turn it down

7 What should you do if the heater is unplugged and the room is cold?
A Plug it in and switch it on **B** Switch it off and unplug it

6 You saw on page 29 of the Student's Book that we can use *keep* + *-ing* to talk about problems that happen every time you try to use equipment and *need* + *-ing* to say what must be done. Rewrite the following sentences in your notebook using *keep* and *need*.

1 The paper jams all the time in the printer.
The paper in the printer keeps jamming.

2 Someone must change the toner in the photocopier.
3 The photocopier always overheats.
4 Someone must clean the computer keyboard.
5 The buttons on the machine jam nearly every day.

Systems and processes

Grammar 1

The following sentences talk about procedures. Change them to the passive form so that the focus of attention is on the procedure, rather than on the person who does it.

1 We update the website every six months.

   The website is updated every six months.

2 We inspect the bathrooms every three hours.

   ....

3 We keep previous invoices in the filing cabinet.

   ....

4 They pay the staff on the last working day of the month.

   ....

5 We give discounts for all orders over £300.

   ....

6 The security guard checks all the bags.

   .... by ....

7 Staff wear gloves when mixing the oil.

   ....

8 Machines pack the perfume bottles into boxes.

   .... by ....

9 They blow cold air over the mixture to cool it.

   ....

Vocabulary

Complete the following definitions using the correct form of the verb in the box. If you need help, look at the flow chart and the transcript for the listening exercise about Chanel No. 5 on pages 31 and 169 of the Student's Book.

~~to blend~~
to dissolve
to distil
to evaporate
to extract

1 If you mix two things together, you ....blend.... them.
2 If a solid breaks down and becomes part of a liquid, it
   ....
3 If a liquid changes into a gas, it ....
4 If you make a liquid stronger by heating it so that it changes into a gas, and then cooling it, you .... it.
5 If you remove one part from a mixture of different things, you .... it.

Grammar 2

1 Check the following words in your dictionary.
- harvest
- lavender
- steam

2 Now read the following text about a British perfume business and put the verbs in brackets in the correct form, either the present simple active or the present simple passive.

THE LAVENDER FARM

Prior Lavender is one of the largest producers of lavender-based products in the UK. We own a farm of over 50 hectares and a distillery where the lavender oil is produced.

Our products

In the past, picking lavender was a hard and time-consuming job. Now, thanks to modern technology, the lavender **1** ..is..cut... (cut) by machine. Most of it **2** .... (distil) with steam to produce lavender oil. This oil **3** .... (use) to make soaps and perfumes. A small part of the lavender crop **4** .... (not go) to the distillery. Instead, the flowers **5** .... (dry) in a current of warm air. These dried flowers **6** .... (use) to fill pillows and cushions.

In the early days, the farm produced mainly lavender oil. Now, however, we have a much wider product range which **7** .... (include) air and clothes fresheners and a number of luxury bath and shower products. Our products **8** .... (sell) in over 300 outlets in the UK and they **9** .... (export) to more than 15 countries.

Staffing

As a result of this expansion, there has been a large increase in the workforce. Now we **10** .... (employ) over 100 permanent members of staff. In addition, approximately 50 temporary workers **11** .... (take on) during the summer to help with the harvest. Despite this, the company **12** .... (remain) essentially a family business. Our general manager, Charles Prior, is the great-grandson of Thomas Prior, the farm's original founder and several other members of the family **13** .... (work) on the farm.

Distribution and delivery

Grammar

1 The sentences (1–6) below describe some company rules about the use of computers in an office. Circle the best modal verb to complete each sentence.

1 Staff *must not/can/should not* access the Internet, but only for work-related reasons. They certainly *must/must not/don't have to* do online shopping during work hours.

2 Members of staff *should/should not/don't have to* tell anyone else their password.

3 Staff *must/must not/don't have to* use the company screensaver. They can choose another one if they prefer.

4 Staff *should/must not/don't have to* bring their own floppy disks to work, in case they infect the system with a virus.

5 Staff *should/should not/don't have to* place drinks near a computer keyboard.

6 Managers *must/can/can't* monitor use of emails and the Internet but they *must/should not/don't have to* tell staff that they are going to do so. They *must/should not/don't have to* open employees' emails without a valid reason.

In very formal language (e.g. contracts), we often avoid modal verbs. We express the same ideas using passive verbs or adjectives:

> *Staff* **are required to** *give three months' notice.* (= Staff have to give three months' notice.)
>
> *Guests* **are advised to** *avoid this area of the city.* (= Guests should avoid this area of the city.)

2 In each of the following pairs of sentences, complete the second sentence with a modal verb so that it has the same meaning as the first sentence. Sometimes more than one answer is possible.

1 **A** Employees are required to obtain a sicknote from their doctor.
  B Employees ..*must/have to*.. obtain a sicknote from their doctor.

2 **A** Mobile phones are not permitted in the seminar room.
  B You .... take mobile phones into the seminar room.

3 **A** You are advised to discuss holiday plans with your line manager.
  B You .... discuss holiday plans with your line manager.

4 **A** Photos are not required for the application form.
  B You .... include a photo on the application form.

5 **A** The balance is payable within two weeks.
  B You .... pay the balance within two weeks.

6 **A** The competition is not open to employees.
  B Employees .... enter the competition.

Vocabulary

1 In the following sentences (1–8), TWO of the alternatives are possible and one is not. Circle the two alternatives which are possible.

1 'Just .... please, while I transfer your call to my colleague.'
A (hold on)   **B** hold up   **C** (hold the line)

2 – Did you speak to Mr Kozak?
– No, I left a message asking him to ....
A call back   **B** ring back   **C** put back

3 'I don't know the number but I'm sure it will be in the phone ....'
A register   **B** book   **C** directory

4 'Do you know the .... for Venezuela? 00, then what?'
A code   **B** score   **C** number

5 'If I'm not in the office, you can call me on my ....'
A mobile   **B** cell phone   **C** handy

6 (recorded message) 'Good morning. This is the Union Bank telephone service. For credit card enquiries, please .... your 16-digit credit card number.'
A enter   **B** compose   **C** key in

7 'One moment please, while I .... to the accounts department.'
A put you through   **B** send your call   **C** transfer your call

8 'I couldn't get through to her because the line was always ....'
A busy   **B** engaged   **C** occupied

2 The language in the following telephone dialogue is correct, but it does not sound polite. Rewrite it so that it sounds more polite.

A Baron Electronics.
B I want to speak to Mr Rosen.
A He's not here. Give me a message.
B Tell him to phone me as soon as possible.
A Who are you?
B Mr Reinhardt from the Cooperative Bank.
A How do you spell it?
B R-E-I-N-H-A-R-D-T.

UNIT 8 Advertising and marketing

Vocabulary

Complete this crossword.

Across

4 Company design which helps identify its products (4)

6 You may see one of these on a website. (6)

7 Someone who sells the same product as you (10)

11 The percentage that one company has of the total sales for a type of product (6, 5)

12 A small piece of paper used to advertise something (5)

Down

1 A short phrase used in advertising (6)

2 A TV advertisement (10)

3 A large outdoor sign used for advertising (9)

5 The company which sells more of a type of product than any other company (6, 6)

8 Advertising activity during a particular period is an advertising .... (8)

9 How people know about your product because other people talk about it (4, 2, 5)

10 If you don't want to do your advertising yourself, you can hire an advertising .... (6)

Grammar

1 Match each cause in box A with an effect in box B.

A

1 Products are often copied by competitors.
2 Many people are annoyed by uninvited phone calls.
3 A company has to know what consumers will need in the future.
4 All products have a life-cycle.
5 People feel that brands guarantee quality.
6 People tell their friends about both good and bad experiences.

B

a Advertising by telephone is not always effective.
b Word-of-mouth can work for or against a product.
c It can be difficult to make money from new ideas.
d Companies have to continually develop new ones.
e It is important to carry out market research.
f They often continue to buy a particular one.

2 Complete the sentences (1–6) by adding either *because* or *so* and the correct ending from either box A or box B.

1 Products are often copied by competitors
  .so it can be difficult to make money from new ideas.

2 Advertising by telephone is not always effective ....

3 A company has to know what consumers will need in the future

  ....

4 All products have a life-cycle ....

5 People feel that brands guarantee quality ....

6 Word-of-mouth can work for or against a product ....

3 Complete the sentences (1–6) below with either *because, so* or *in order to*.

1 The company decided to change their slogan ...because..... they thought the product needed a new image.

2 They advertised on three different radio stations .... reach a wide range of people.

3 They lowered their prices .... attract a different group of consumers.

4 The company decided to market to existing customers .... they set up a consumer database.

5 .... they could not afford to advertise on TV, they decided to write a commercial for radio.

6 They thought the company needed a new image .... they hired a marketing and design expert.

Making arrangements

Grammar

Look at these headlines and documents, then complete what the people are saying using the verb in brackets in the correct future form.

> **CREDIT NORTH ANNOUNCES PLANS TO CLOSE TORONTO BRANCH**

> ANALYSTS PREDICT 5% FALL IN HOUSE PRICES

Mr Alexander Ionov		
22 Jan:	London Heathrow	08.55
	Moscow Domodedovo	15.45
26 Jan:	Moscow Domodedovo	21.05
	London Heathrow	22.05

Dear Mr Ionov

We confirm your reservation of a single room at the Moscow President Hotel for 4 nights, 22 to 25 Jan inclusive.

Hayley: TO DO LIST

1 Urgent: check payroll for this month

2 Ring Karen re invoice

We **1** .....are going to close.... (close) our branch in Toronto.

Managing director of Credit North

I **2** .... (fly) to Moscow on 22 January and I **3** .... (come) back to London on 26 January. I **4** .... (stay) at the President Hotel for four nights.

Alexander Ionov

What **5** .... you .... (do) today, Hayley?

Well, first of all, I **6** .... (check) the payroll.

Our prediction is that house prices **7** .... (fall) by 5 per cent before the end of the year.

James Rowe, financial analyst

Vocabulary

It is difficult to know whether a word or expression is used with the verb *make* or *do*. The table below shows some common collocations.

Make	Do
an appointment	business with someone
a deal*	a deal*
a decision	homework
a meal	some research
a mistake	some work
an offer	someone a favour
a phone call	well
a plan	your best

*It is possible to say both *do a deal* and *make a deal* with no real difference in meaning.

1 Complete the following text, using *make* or *do* in the correct tense and form.

Yesterday was a busy day. I went into work early because there was a lot of paperwork that I had to **1** .... do........... . I couldn't finish it all because at eleven o'clock I met a client who **2** .... an offer to buy a large quantity of one of our products. We agreed on the price and he **3** .... a decision about the exact quantity before the end of the week.

In the afternoon, I had to **4** .... some phone calls and carry on with the paperwork. My colleague helped me but he is new and still sometimes **5** .... mistakes with the forms. I also managed to ring the dentist and I **6** .... an appointment for a check-up next week.

In the evening, I **7** .... supper for my son and I helped him **8** .... his homework. I think he **9** .... well at school at the moment. Finally, I went to bed feeling very tired.

2 Add any other expressions you know with *make* or *do* to the chart above.

UNIT 10 Transport

Vocabulary 1

1 In each gap in the following dialogues (1–7), write either a compound noun or a collocation. If you need help, look at page 46 in your Student's Book.

(At the check-in)

1 **A** Can I keep this bag with me as well?
   B I'm afraid not. We only allow one piece of ..hand .luggage... per passenger.

2 **A** This is your .... , sir. You need gate number 14. Please be there half an hour before departure time.
   B Thank you.

3 **A** That's by the window. Is that all right, sir?
   B Well, actually I'd prefer an .... if you've got one. I like the extra space for my legs.

4 **A** I'm afraid I forgot to order a vegetarian meal.
   B Well, they often have one or two extra. If you tell the .... as soon as you .... , they'll probably be able to help you.

(On the plane)

5 **A** Excuse me, do you mind if we .... ? Then I can be next to my colleague.
   B No, not at all.

6 **A** I'm afraid you can't put your bag there, madam, because it's blocking the .... You'll have to put it in the ....
   B Oh, OK.

7 **A** I'm looking forward to some nice warm weather.
   B Yes, it was so cold this morning. Look at me in this thick jacket. I'm going to be so hot when we ....

2 What happens when you take a plane trip? Match the beginnings (1–8) and endings (a–h) of these sentences.

1 You put   a your bags.
2 You receive   b a boarding card.
3 You check in   c takes off.
4 You fasten   d the security check.
5 You board   e the plane.
6 You go through   f your seatbelt.
7 You show   g your hand luggage in the locker.
8 The plane   h your passport and boarding card.

3 Write the sentences from Exercise 2 in the correct order in your notebook.

Grammar

Complete the following text by putting one of the contrast words from the box in each gap. Use each one once only.

<table>
<tr><td>although</td></tr>
<tr><td>but</td></tr>
<tr><td>despite</td></tr>
<tr><td>however</td></tr>
</table>

In the past, travel managers reduced their company's travel expenses by asking for discounted prices with an airline **1** ..b̲u̲t̲.. now this is starting to change. The rise of the budget airline means that employees and travel managers often find very cheap flights over the Internet. The airlines themselves have started to respond to this. **2** .... budget airlines do not usually offer high levels of customer care, some of them have started to offer a business class service.

3 .... , these low-cost airlines have a number of disadvantages. There is often no compensation if the flight is cancelled. Changing the time of your flight can often be expensive, too. **4** .... the higher cost of tickets, the best option for many companies is still a corporate rate with a traditional airline.

Vocabulary 2

Read the following information (1–3) about the rail industry and try to work out the meaning of the words in bold type. Write an approximate meaning for each at the bottom of the page. The link words in *italics* will help you.

1 This used to be a very poor region *but* since the new rail link was built, the tourist industry has really **prospered**.
2 The cost of repairing the railway line was estimated at €3 billion, *but* in fact it **exceeded** this because the railway was in a worse condition than people thought.
3 The market share of many rail passenger services has **plunged**, *because* low-cost airlines can offer cheaper fares. *However*, high-speed trains such as Japan's 'Shinkansen' and France's 'Trains à Grande Vitesse' have nearly always **withstood** competition from other forms of transport.

- prospered   ....
- exceeded   ....
- plunged   ....
- withstood   ....

UNIT 11 Business accommodation

Vocabulary

1 The following webpage advertises accommodation in London. Read it and choose alternatives for the words in *italics* from the box. There are three words more than you need.

HOMEBOOKERS

We have over 200 apartments and houses for rent. For the business traveller, we are the alternative to characterless hotels. Our homes are

1 *attractively* [tastefully] furnished and fully equipped with bedlinen, towels, crockery, cutlery, etc. They are **2** *within easy reach of* the city centre. Minimum stay is seven nights.

Payment

We require full payment six weeks **3** *prior to* arrival. If you need to cancel the **4** *booking*, we can only supply a refund if we are able to re-let the property. For this reason, we advise you to **5** *take out* travel insurance. If you need to change your date of arrival or **6** *prolong* your stay, please contact us immediately. We also require a deposit of £200.

Arrival and departure

If you are arriving in London by plane or train, we **7** *suggest* that you hire one of our drivers. He or she will have the keys to the property and be able to drive you straight there in comfort. On the day of your departure, you are required to **8** *vacate* the property by midday.

To view possible areas of London, **click here**.

after
arrive
before
conveniently
extend
leave
not far from
obtain
recommend
reservation
~~tastefully~~

---

2 Write any collocations that you want to remember in your notebook. You may want to list collocations with similar meanings together (e.g. *attractively/tastefully furnished*).

Writing

1 Circle the correct alternative, A or B, to create an email to Homebookers.

1 **A** *I would like* (circled) **B** *I need*	2 **A** *renting* **B** *to rent*	a one-bedroom apartment in London from 12
3 **A** *to 21 July,* **B** *and 21 July,*	preferably	4 **A** *in the area of* **B** *in the quarter of* Chelsea.
5 **A** *You send me* **B** *Please could you send me*		details of some possible properties?
6 **A** *Do you also offer* **B** *Are you also offering*		a cleaning service?
7 **A** *Kind regards,* **B** *Over and out,* Sahar Al-Hussein		

2 Match the phrases in columns A–C to make a reply of four sentences to Sahar Al-Hussein. Then write the sentences in your notebook in the correct order.

A	B	C
I attach details	we can provide contact details	as demand is high.
Although we do not run a cleaning service,	to book as soon as possible	regarding booking an apartment.
Thank you for your email	of suitable apartments	which are available on the dates you require.
I would advise you	of 3 June	of local cleaning agencies.

UNIT 12 Out of the office

Grammar

Below you will find feedback forms from two delegates. These were given in at the end of the conference that you heard about in the listening exercise on page 56 of the Student's Book.

Delegate A

	poor	satisfactory	good	very good
Stefania Volksmann		✓		
Rachel Tebbit			✓	
Tim Shi				✓
Dr Dieter Pietsch			✓	
Alan Rolfe			✓	
Discussion panel	✓			
Location			✓	
Conference staff				✓

Comments: Mr Shi's talk v. useful, but not a good room – too small.
Rachel Tebbit was also interesting.
Least interesting part was discussion panel – too long and boring.
Conference staff v. helpful, unlike last year!

Delegate B

	poor	satisfactory	good	very good
Stefania Volksmann		✓		
Rachel Tebbit			✓	
Tim Shi			✓	
Dr Dieter Pietsch				✓
Alan Rolfe			✓	
Discussion panel			✓	
Location		✓		
Conference staff			✓	

Comments: Dr Pietsch's session really good, and great fun! Mr Rolfe also useful but a bit serious.
Hotel rather far from centre. Why not same hotel as last year?
2 hours not enough for discussion panel.

Study the forms and complete the following sentences (1–8) with either a comparative or a superlative form. Use each adjective from the box once only.

dull	1 Delegate A thinks that Rachel Tebbit's talk was ~~more interesting~~. than Stefania Volksmann's.
entertaining	
~~good~~	2 Delegate B thinks that Dr Pietsch's talk was ~~the best~~. .
useful	3 Delegate A thinks that Tim Shi's session was .... of all.
helpful	4 Delegate A thinks that Tim Shi's session needed a .... room.
~~interesting~~	
large	5 Delegate A thinks that the discussion panel was .... part.
long	

6 Delegate B thinks that it is a pity that the discussion panel was not ....

7 Delegate A thinks that the conference staff were .... than last year.

8 Delegate B thinks that Dr Pietsch was .... than Mr Rolfe.

Vocabulary

1 Match the verbs in column A with objects in column B to make collocations about organising or attending a conference. Some verbs can go with more than one object.

A	B
wear	a presentation
give	the venue
put up	a feedback form
attend	a badge
book	a lecture
give out	information packs
fill in	signs

2 Who would normally do each of the actions in the list above? Record each collocation in the correct column below. One action would normally be done by all three types of people.

A delegate	A speaker	An organiser
attend a lecture		

13 Developing contacts

Grammar

Complete the following profile of a company manager, putting the verbs in brackets in either the past simple or the present perfect.

JIM BLAKE

Jim Blake **1** .... joined ... (join) Hodson Electricals in 1980, immediately after finishing his degree in chemical engineering. In 1988, the company **2** .... (choose) him to run the consumer products division. Then, in 1995, Jim's strong performance **3** .... (earn) him the top job. He **4** .... (become) CEO of Hodson Electrics at the age of just 46.

Since then, Jim's career **5** .... (be) an example of how to manage a company successfully. For the last ten years, Hodson Electrics **6** .... (expand) continually and now it **7** .... (become) one of the most highly valued companies in Europe. One of Jim's secrets is to develop talented people. Recently, he **8** .... (establish) a series of performance measures that identify who the best performers are. Executives are now promoted without regard to seniority. For example, when he had to choose a new Chief Financial Officer two years ago, Blake **9** .... (pass) over several candidates in favour of 38-year-old Ben Bradley. He **10** .... (insist) always, 'Age doesn't matter. It's your ability that counts'.

People **11** .... (call) Blake many things during his career but one thing that nobody can call him is lazy. His energy and enthusiasm **12** .... (make) the company what it is today.

Reading

Read the extract opposite from a book that gives advice about networking. Write the correct paragraph heading (a–g) from the list below above each paragraph (1–7).

a Follow up
b ~~Develop a networking attitude~~
c Have fun, but be polite
d Everyone's favourite word
e Circulate
f Be friendly and show interest
g Take the first step

NETWORKING STRATEGIES

1 .b.. Take the opportunity to build up new contacts whenever you are in business or social situations. Don't just talk to your friends and colleagues.

2 ...... At parties, don't stay in one position. Move around the room so that you talk to as many people as possible.

3 ...... Be the first to introduce yourself to others, especially to successful people who have a wide range of contacts.

4 ...... Repeat the person's name when you first meet them and use it during the conversation, especially at the end.

5 ...... People do business with people that they like and trust. The sooner you build up trust and try to help others, the faster your networking will produce results in terms of referrals and contracts.

6 ...... It is easy to make a good impression but it is also easy to put people off. One joke in bad taste or an offensive comment can destroy the chances for future business.

7 ...... Keep in touch with the people you meet. Send an email after the event to say how much you enjoyed meeting them and that you hope to see them again.

Vocabulary

Now choose five useful verb–noun collocations from the text and write them below.

....

....

....

....

....

UNIT 14 Cultural issues

Grammar

Complete this text about meetings in different countries by putting one of the phrases from the box into each gap.

WHAT ARE YOUR MEETINGS LIKE?

Most companies hold meetings but they can be organised in different ways and have very different purposes. Different countries also have different ideas about how to run a meeting.

a	are not normally made
b	tend to discuss
c	~~will often come~~
d	do not generally like
e	usually make
f	normally makes
g	usually take place
h	are normally seen
i	tends to be

Most meetings have an agenda, that is, a written list of things to be discussed. In Germany, this is usually very important. People prepare for the meeting carefully and **1** ..c.. to the meeting with statements and reports which relate to particular items on the agenda. For this reason, German business people **2** ...... changing the agenda at all. This contrasts with some other countries like France or the UK, where people sometimes change items on the agenda at the beginning of the meeting. In France, people also **3** ...... different issues together, instead of talking about one thing at a time.

The purpose of a meeting is also different in different cultures. In Germany, people **4** ...... decisions in meetings, whereas in France meetings **5** ...... as a place to share information and make suggestions. The boss **6** ...... the final decision after the meeting. In some Southern European countries, such as Italy or Greece, people often favour informal places for discussions. What is said in the bar or over lunch **7** ...... just as important as what is said in a meeting. In Japan, too, decisions **8** ...... in a meeting. All the discussions **9** ...... before the meeting, sometimes out of the office. The meeting is the place to announce officially what has already been decided.

Vocabulary

You can make the opposite of many words by adding a **prefix** (syllable at the beginning of the word). The most common prefix for this is *un-*:

happy → *unhappy*   *able* → *unable*

1 Add a prefix to the adjectives on the next page to make opposites. In most cases you need to add *un-*, but there are three adjectives which need a different prefix. Look at the text on page 65 in the Student's Book if you need help.

Adjective	Opposite
lucky	
fortunate	
successful	
formal	
polite	
friendly	
patient	
comfortable	
clear	
popular	
common	
likely	
usual	
official	

2 Choose a suitable word with a negative prefix from the table above to complete the following sentences.

1 The company's attempt to break into the Asian market was ....

2 They have not published the sales figures yet, but .... estimates say that they will probably be 5 per cent down on last year.

3 The administrative changes in the company were very .... with staff.

3 Add other examples of words with negative prefixes to the table as you learn them.

Teamwork

Vocabulary

Many nouns can be formed by adding **suffixes** (e.g. *-ation* and *-ment*) to verbs.

1 Add the correct suffix to the following verbs to form nouns. Some of the
   answers are in the text on team-building activities on page 67 of the
   Student's Book. Use a dictionary only if necessary.

Verb	Noun
organise	organisation
arrange	
communicate	
appreciate	
equip	

Suffixes can also be used to form adjectives:

Verb/noun	Adjective
rely	reli**able**
create	crea**tive**
entertain	entertain**ing**
industry	industri**al**

Note how words ending in *e* drop the final *e* before forming the adjective
with *-ive* (e.g. *create/creative*) and words ending in *consonant* + *y* change
the *y* to an *i*, (e.g. *rely/reliable*).

---

2 Add suffixes to the following verbs to make nouns and adjectives. You
   will find some of the answers on page 67 of the Student's Book.

Verb	Noun	Adjective
entertain		
excite		
attract		
enjoy		
protect		
benefit		

3 Complete the sentences (1–5) at the top of the next page with a word
   formed from the verb in brackets.

1 The treasure hunt was very entertaining (entertain) but I'm not sure if it was very profitable.

2 Many thanks for such an .... (enjoy) event.

3 The team came up with a number of .... (attract) suggestions.

4 This is one of the most .... (excite) projects we have worked on.

5 Please accept this small gift as a token (= *sign*) of our .... (appreciate).

Writing

1 It is very important to check your writing for spelling mistakes. The following email was written to the organiser of the chocolate workshop described on page 67 of the Student's Book. Read it and identify eight spelling mistakes. Write the correct spellings on the right.

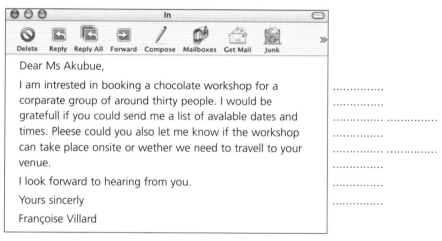

Dear Ms Akubue,

I am intrested in booking a chocolate workshop for a corparate group of around thirty people. I would be gratefull if you could send me a list of avalable dates and times. Pleese could you also let me know if the workshop can take place onsite or wether we need to travell to your venue.

I look forward to hearing from you.

Yours sincerly

Françoise Villard

....
....
....
....
....
....
....
....
....

2 Match the two halves of the sentences in the letter below. Then write the sentences in a suitable order in your notebook to create a reply to Françoise Villard.

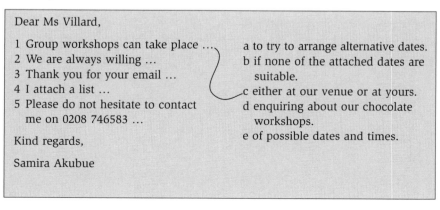

Dear Ms Villard,

1 Group workshops can take place ...
2 We are always willing ...
3 Thank you for your email ...
4 I attach a list ...
5 Please do not hesitate to contact me on 0208 746583 ...

Kind regards,

Samira Akubue

a to try to arrange alternative dates.
b if none of the attached dates are suitable.
c either at our venue or at yours.
d enquiring about our chocolate workshops.
e of possible dates and times.

Entertaining clients

Grammar

1 Read the following article and divide the words in bold type into two groups, according to whether they are *countable* or *uncountable* in the text. If you are not sure, look at the Grammar workshop on page 70 of the Student's Book. Be careful, as one or two of the words can be countable or uncountable according to the context.

BUON CAFFÉ

The coffee shop Buon Caffé opened 16 new outlets in the first quarter, and recorded a sales **increase** of 5.6%. According to Armando Cherici, chief executive, the growth in **revenue** has been enough to speed up the company's expansion programme. They will now have over 20 stores by next February.

Buon Caffé started in 1992 with a small coffee shop in West London. It soon became famous for its Italian **coffee** and high quality **food**. Part of its secret was the use of Italian **bread** and quality fresh ingredients for every sandwich but their success was also thanks to their investment in top quality **equipment** to produce the coffee. Staff were trained in how to use a **grinder** and an espresso **machine** correctly. The shop also provided customers with forms so that they could give **feedback** on the Buon Caffé experience. The result was rapid growth and 14 more Buon Caffé shops were opened in the next 10 years. It now takes just three months for a new Buon Caffé shop to start making a **profit**.

There is **evidence** to suggest that in London the coffee shop is starting to take over from the pub as a place where people meet for social or business purposes. Market **research** carried out on a group of 18-to 24-year-olds found that 48% of them went to the coffee shop for their lunch break and over 50% preferred it as a place to meet clients. If so, there is probably plenty of **room** for Buon Caffé to grow further.

Countable	Uncountable
increase	revenue

2 Correct the mistakes in the following sentences.

1 The project did not make as ~~many~~ money as we hoped. ..much...

2 We really need to get some feedbacks from our customers. ....

3 There are not many evidences to suggest that our clientele is getting younger. ....

4 We are going to replace all of these equipments. ....

5 All of these informations need to be entered into the computer. ....

Writing

Read these phrases from two short thank you letters. One is formal and the other informal. Put the phrases together in the right order to create two separate letters.

to make the event a success

your very entertaining lecture

was the most interesting of the conference.

to her as well

~~Dear Mr Kitson~~

at the conference last week

From Tony and Sarah

I am writing to thank you for

and please pass on our thanks

was almost entirely positive

It was lovely to meet Barbara

and a large number of delegates said that your lecture

The feedback that we received about the event

for the wonderful meal last night

Thank you again for helping

Thanks very much

Yours sincerely

~~Dear Robert~~

Jonathon Gabriel

A

Dear Mr Kitson,

B

Dear Robert,

17 Describing statistics

Grammar

The following line graph shows the unemployment rate (percentage of the workforce who are unemployed) in Indonesia for the period 1990 to 2004.

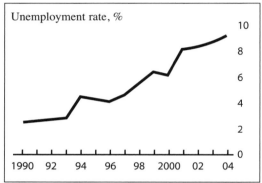

The Economist

1 Read the following description of the graph.

In 1990, the unemployment rate stood at just over 2 per cent. *There was a slight rise* over the next three years and then in 1993, *it increased sharply* to over 4 per cent. During the next two years *it fell slightly*, but then it increased again to reach over 6 per cent at the beginning of 1999. After that, *there was another dip*, but then *it rose dramatically*. The rate hit 8 per cent in 2001. *There was a more gradual rise* over the following three years.

2 Write an alternative version in your notebook, changing the verb–adverb phrases in italics to nouns and adjectives and vice versa. Begin with the sentences below.

In 1990, the unemployment rate stood at just over 2 per cent.
It rose slightly over the next three years and then in 1993,
there was a sharp increase to over 4 per cent.

....

3 Circle the correct alternative in *italics* to complete the following text.

STRONG SALES AT IBIS GROUP

Ibis group reported a **1** *successful/successfully* second quarter of trading yesterday with overall sales 3.5 per cent higher than the same period last year. Bonaccord, the flagship fashion outlet, performed very well with a **2** *steady/steadily* rise in profits from £10.2 million in 2005 to £12.3 million in 2006. The women's clothing department performed very **3** *strong/strongly* and sales were also helped by the **4** *recent/recently* refurbishment of twenty of their stores. Sales also rose **5** *sharp/sharply* at Fragrance, the perfume store which the group acquired in September.

It must be admitted that the figures for Bertrand, the group's fashion outlet for the over-50s, **6** *complete/completely* failed to reflect this success. Here, like-for-like profits fell by 4.1 per cent. However, this poor performance was not **7** *unexpected/ unexpectedly* and was partly caused by the wet weather which affected the sales of summer clothes. Mr Tim Wright, chief executive, is **8** *confident/confidently* that things will improve.

Vocabulary

Below you will find two mixed-up descriptions of the movements in the share prices of two different companies over a week. Separate the two descriptions by choosing A or B for 1–5 in the box below. Write the two descriptions below.

1 **A** The share price rose slightly on Monday and continued …	**B** The share price showed a slight fall on Monday and continued …
2 **A** … to go down the following day. However, …	**B** … to climb the following day. However, …
3 **A** Wednesday saw an end to this downward trend as the price stabilised.	**B** Wednesday saw an end to this upward trend as the price levelled off.
4 **A** There were no further increases on Thursday either but unfortunately on Friday …	**B** There were no further drops in price on Thursday either but on Friday there was a complete change of fortune as …
5 **A** … the price suddenly recovered and rose sharply to exceed even Monday's value.	**B** … the price suddenly plunged to just below Monday's value.

Company X

1   The share price rose slightly on Monday and continued
    to climb the following day. However,

Company Y

1   The share price showed a slight fall on Monday and continued
    to go down the following day. However,

18 Company finances

Vocabulary

1 Look at this profit and loss account for Supersox, a company which makes socks. Read the sentences (a–h) and write the correct figures in the profit and loss account.

SUPERSOX

Profit and Loss Account

November 2006

Sales income	1 .27,150.........
Cost of sales	
Labour	2 ....
Stock movement	3 ....
Distribution	4 ....
Gross profit	19,650
Overheads	
Personnel	5 ....
Building costs	6 ....
Stationery and publications	217
Telephone	850
Computer costs	7 ....
Advertising	1,000
Depreciation*	8 ....
Total overheads	17,597
Net profit/loss	+ 2,053

---

* the reduction in value of an asset over a period of time

In November 2006:

a The total salaries of staff not involved with production (e.g. administrative staff) were £7,540.

b The company used raw materials to the value of £750 to make their products.

c The company spent £840 on new software.

d The company spent £810 on delivering their products.

e The company earned a total of £27,150 from selling the socks.

f The company paid their production staff £5,940 in salaries.

g The estimated fall in value of the company's assets was £1,000.

h They paid £6,100 rent for their office and factory.

2 Complete the following definition.

The net profit or loss is calculated by subtracting the **1** .... from the **2** ....

3 Find twelve finance words in the word square. They can be written across, down or diagonally. Three words are written backwards. The clues below will help you.

r	r	t	d	w	l	o	s	s
e	e	u	e	o	c	q	d	s
v	a	r	b	l	r	a	e	o
e	n	n	t	f	e	s	f	r
n	h	o	o	h	d	s	i	g
u	t	v	r	s	i	e	c	p
e	n	e	t	a	t	t	i	k
f	v	r	m	c	o	d	t	p
o	b	a	n	k	r	u	p	t

1 Someone who a company must pay money to

2 Someone who owes money to a company (the opposite of **1**)

3 The total sales of a company over a particular period

4 Another word for the money that a company receives over a particular period

5 Rent, electricity bills and administrative costs are all examples of ....

6 The opposite of a profit

7 If a company cannot continue because it is losing money it goes ....

8 The money a company makes *before* deducting the running costs and taxes is the .... profit

9 The money a company makes *after* deducting the running costs and taxes is the .... profit

10 The amount of money that a company has lost

11 The amount of money going into and coming out of a company

12 Something valuable that a company owns, like land or machinery

UNIT 19 Investments

Grammar

1 Write the effect (1–4) next to the correct cause in the table below.

1 They are over before investors can take advantage of them
2 They buy more in winter
3 It is difficult to predict
4 People buy less in the summer

Cause	Effect
In December people often feel positive about the New Year	
People are on holiday in July and August	
The stock market is influenced by many different things	
Big gains in share prices usually happen very suddenly	

2 Now complete the following text with the link words from the box below. If you have difficulty, look again at page 41 (cause and effect words) and page 49 (contrast words) in the Student's Book. You need to use two words twice.

SEASONAL CHANGES IN SHARE PRICES

There is some evidence that stock markets give better returns at certain times of the year. The traditional idea is that share prices rise in the winter 1 ....*but*.... then they fall in the summer. One obvious explanation of this is that people buy less in the summer 2 .... they are on holiday in July and August. In December, people often feel positive about the New Year 3 .... they buy more.

4 .... , most financial advisers do not advise trying to follow seasonal changes in the stock market. The stock market is much more difficult to predict than this 5 .... it is affected by so many different things, like wars and natural disasters. In addition, the really big gains in share prices usually happen very quickly 6 .... they are over before investors can take advantage of them. It is more important to invest for the long term than to try to predict the stock market's every move.

| so   because   ~~but~~   however |

Vocabulary

Complete the crossword below.

Across

6 The collection of shares that someone has (9)

8 A market where share prices are rising is a .... market (4)

9 A company which is at least 51% owned by another is a ....
company (10)

10 Part of the money invested in a business (5)

11 The action of making shares available to the public for the first time (9)

12 The result of joining two companies together (6)

13 The part of the company profits which is paid to shareholders (8)

Down

1 Money which is used for investment (7)

2 Profits made from investments (7)

3 A certain quantity of shares (5)

4 Oil, gold and coffee are all examples of .... (11)

5 Someone who can buy and sell shares for you (6)

7 If you don't want to invest in shares, you might invest in these (5)

8 A market where share prices are falling is a .... market (4)

Grammar

1 The following is part of an article about Parker Brothers, a famous American manufacturer of games. Read the account of how they started up and put *who* or *which* in each gap.

PARKER BROTHERS

Parker Brothers is now a subsidiary of the toy giant Hasbro, but it is still a highly valued brand with a logo which is known throughout the world.

The company started up in the 1880s. George Parker was an enterprising teenager **1** .who. lived in Salem, Massachusetts. He loved playing different board games with his brothers and friends and formed a special club where they could meet for *this purpose*. Although there were a few board games at that time, most of them were designed to teach moral or religious values. George was not very interested in *these*, so at the age of 16, he invented 'Banking', a game **2** .... was about becoming rich through investments. The members of the club enjoyed it so much that they suggested that George should try to sell it. He offered it to two book publishers **3** .... refused it. Unwilling to give up, George borrowed $50 from his friends and used *this* to produce 500 versions of *the game*. He then went off to sell these around Salem and Boston, the two towns **4** .... he knew best. He returned home with a profit of $100.

This capital was used to set up George S. Parker Company in downtown Salem. George's two brothers soon joined *the enterprise* and it expanded rapidly. By 1888, its catalogue listed 29 games. The most popular games were often those **5** .... were invented by George himself.

One of the most successful board games in the history of *the industry* is 'Monopoly', so it is interesting that George Parker never liked *this one* very much. It was first created in the 1930s by Charles Darrow, **6** .... offered it to the Parker brothers. George, however, rejected it, saying that no one would want to buy a game **7** .... took so long to play. *Its inventor* then did exactly what George had done nearly fifty years previously — produced the game *himself* and sold it locally. It did so well that Parker Brothers were quickly forced to reconsider. In 1935, they acquired 'Monopoly' and it very soon became a global success.

2 Look at the words and expressions in *italics* in the text about the Parker Brothers. Each of them refers to someone or something else in the text. Write what each one refers to.

1 The company ....Parker..Brothers.

2 this purpose ....

3 these ....

4 this ....

5 the game ....

6 This capital ....

7 the enterprise ....

8 the industry ....

9 this one ....

10 Its inventor ....

11 himself ....

Vocabulary

1 Circle the correct verb in the sentences below (1–8).

1 Your business plan shows that it will be difficult to *(cover)/wrap/lay* the running costs.

2 The government have *rained/poured/dripped* a lot of money into this project.

3 They *got out/took out/made out* a loan to buy three new company vans.

4 The global vehicle market is preparing for a *flood/river/ocean* of new imports from Asia.

5 They had no assets which they could use to *back up/back down/back off* the loan.

6 The bank refused to give us a loan, so it was difficult to *raise/carry/lift* the money to start the business.

7 We have *invested/spent/lent* a great deal of time and money in this idea.

8 We have such a small profit margin that we really have to find ways of *breaking/cutting/tearing* costs.

2 Write the correct collocations below to help you remember them.

....

....

....

....

....

....

....

....

21 Job applications

Vocabulary

1 In the following exercise, you have to change adjectives to nouns. Two of the most common suffixes for this are *-ness* and *-ity*. Complete the table, being careful to think about any necessary spelling changes. If you need help, look at the sentences (1–5) below.

Adjective	Noun
punctual	punctuality
polite	
rude	
generous	generosity
kind	
sincere	sincerity
original	
courteous	
reliable	
creative	
sensitive	
loyal	

2 Read the following statements (1–5) taken from references for job applicants. Decide whether an adjective or a noun is the correct word in each case.

1 Harriet is an extremely *reliable*/*reliability* member of staff and has shown *flexible*/*flexibility* about working extra hours at weekends.

2 Khaled has introduced a number of *original*/*originality* measures to try to reduce staff costs and his energy and *creative*/*creativity* have been much appreciated.

3 The department has taken on a number of new members of staff this year and Hiroko has played a key role in helping them. A number of them have commented positively on her *helpful*/*helpfulness* and *courteous*/*courtesy*.

4 Michael has been a *loyal*/*loyalty* and long-standing member of the company and colleagues have often seen him as a source of *stable*/*stability* in difficult times.

5 Mohan has considerable expertise in managing difficult situations and shows both *sensitive*/*sensitivity* and skill in dealing with staff.

3 The phrases in list A are taken from job advertisements and describe the skills that a successful candidate must have. The phrases in list B are taken from the personal profile section of different CVs.

Match each skill in list A with one in list B.

A

1 You need the ability to use your initiative.
2 The successful candidate will have good interpersonal skills.
3 You must be PC literate.
4 You need to show attention to detail.
5 You must show good time-management.
6 You must be committed to lifelong learning.
7 The successful candidate will be able to cope with uncertainty.
8 You must be a good team player.

B

a I have good computer skills.
b I always welcome opportunities for further training and development.
c I work well in a group.
d I am able to organise my work timetable and meet deadlines.
e I am able to work and take decisions independently.
f I am able to complete tasks with precision and accuracy.
g I can form good relationships with many different people.
h I can adapt to changing circumstances and take calculated risks.

4 Now record the noun form of the following adjectives. The answers are in the exercise above.

Adjective	Noun	
precise		
accurate		
certain (think!)		

Recruitment

Grammar

1 The text below contains a number of first conditional sentences. Put one of the *if* clauses from the box below in each gap.

DISABLED STAFF

1 ..c... , most people will think you mean avoiding racial or sexual discrimination. However, there are other types of discrimination too. True diversity means making sure that no group of people is prevented from being a member of your staff because of prejudice.*

Disabled workers are one such group. When we think of a disabled person, we often think of someone with mobility problems who needs to use a wheelchair, but there are other types of disability too, like sight or hearing problems.

Disabled staff have skills and experience which can benefit your business. **2** .... , this will increase the range of candidates for recruiting staff. On the other hand, **3** .... , you may discourage the right person for the job. Not only that, but reports suggest that disabled staff are often very good at creative thinking. This is not surprising, as most of them have to come up with creative solutions to help them in their day-to-day lives. **4** .... , for example, you are likely to be an excellent problem-solver.

The changes needed in the workplace for disabled people are often quite small. You may need to make minor changes to the building and possibly some other changes, depending on the type of disability. For example, **5** .... , company documents may be needed in a different format, like a recording or in large print.

Finally, it is worth remembering that **6** .... , you will probably attract a more diverse range of customers. After all, most disabled people could be your customers as well.

* an unfair or unreasonable feeling against a group of people

a if you are a wheelchair-user who has to travel on the railway
b if you employ someone with sight problems
c ~~if you mention diversity~~
d if disabled people feel they cannot apply
e if you are willing to consider employing a disabled person
f if you have a diverse workforce

2 Complete the following conversation by writing either *will* or *would* in each gap.

A I think we'll have to take on another administrative assistant.

B Do we really need an extra person? Just ask Leila if she wants to do one or two extra hours.

A I'm sure she doesn't. She does too much already.

B Do you think she **1** ..would.. say 'no' even if it was only one or two hours?

A It's more than that.

B But the problem is that sometimes there's a lot of extra paperwork, but sometimes there's very little. I think if I were you, I **2** .... just get some temporary staff in for those times. If you contacted the agency, I'm sure they **3** .... find someone.

A I haven't always been very happy with the quality of people that the agency have sent us. At least if we interview the person ourselves, we **4** .... have a better idea about how suitable they are.

B And do you think you can persuade the human resources department to take on a permanent new member of staff?

A Well, I'm going to try. If I produce a report and a proposed job description, I think they **5** .... accept the idea.

Vocabulary

Complete the following story of how someone lost their job, using the correct word from the box. You will need one word more than once.

Last week, I was an engineer in a telecommunications company. This week I am **1** ..unemployed. !

I heard about the job just after I **2** .... from university. I sent in my **3** .... and, after a short interview, they offered me the position. Ironically, I **4** .... two other job offers later that week.

After just one month, the **5** .... manager called me into her office and told me that the company's sales were much lower than forecast and they had to **6** .... staff. It was 'last in, first out', so I was made **7** .... – I received just one month's **8** .... pay.

I still feel shocked of course, but they say this is a good time for a **9** .... to seek employment, so I'm fairly sure I'll find something else soon. I've updated my **10** .... and have started looking through the **11** .... again.

curriculum vitae
graduate
graduated
human resources
lay off
newspaper ads
redundancy
redundant
turned down
~~unemployed~~

UNIT 23 Staff development

Vocabulary

Find twelve words or verbs + preposition associated with human resources in the word square. They can be written horizontally or vertically, but not backwards. Use the clues below to help you.

p	a	m	m	c	w	z	m	l	p	n	y	p
g	p	s	x	r	h	r	e	f	e	r	e	e
s	p	r	v	l	f	o	i	f	r	c	e	q
h	r	é	j	w	l	i	z	z	s	b	l	o
o	a	s	j	t	o	w	k	o	o	p	c	n
r	i	u	s	u	g	g	f	t	n	y	n	u
t	s	m	q	i	p	y	y	o	n	t	o	a
l	a	é	l	a	y	o	f	f	e	d	t	p
i	l	k	c	j	d	t	j	g	l	o	i	v
s	f	l	p	r	o	m	o	t	e	p	c	h
t	w	o	r	k	f	o	r	c	e	b	e	b
d	i	s	m	i	s	s	v	h	b	p	j	o
y	a	u	j	y	x	r	e	t	i	r	e	r
d	q	w	t	u	r	n	d	o	w	n	n	c

1 A US word for 'CV'
2 If you give someone a job in a higher position, you .... them
3 A phrasal verb meaning 'make redundant'
4 The people who work in a company or organisation
5 If people think you are one of the most suitable applicants for a job, you are put on the ....
6 If you remove someone from their job, you .... them
7 The person who gives you a reference
8 If you resign from your job, you hand in your ....
9 A report on an employee which gives details about their performance
10 A phrasal verb, meaning 'reject someone' (for a job)
11 Stop work because of old age
12 Another word for 'staff'.

Grammar

The following text is taken from a guide to doing staff appraisals. The words in *italics* are in the wrong form (for example a verb is written instead of a noun or an adjective instead of an adverb). Read the text and change the words in *italics* to the correct form.

Staff appraisals are very important. They can make the difference between a committed, successful team and a personnel disaster. However, they can also be tricky to get right. Here are some basic guidelines.

➡ Set a time and date for the appraisal and stick to it.

➡ Appraisals are an opportunity to discuss the employee's
performance
1 ~~perform~~ so don't be tempted to start discussing other issues.

➡ Try to get an objective view of the employee's **2** *perform* by asking other members of the **3** *manage* team for their opinions too.

➡ Don't take calls or allow **4** *interrupt* during the appraisal. This shows that you take the procedure **5** *serious*.

➡ Listen to the employee. Don't talk too much yourself, even if you think that your superior **6** *know* can solve the employee's problems.

➡ Don't give only **7** *criticise*. If the appraisal is too negative, the employee may become **8** *demotivation*.

➡ Appraisals can also be too positive, so that the employee thinks 'I am so good, there is nothing I need to **9** *improvement*.' You can **10** *avoidance* both of these traps by using the company standards and the job description to **11** *measurement* how well the employee is doing.

➡ Write up the results **12** *prompt*.

Staff facts and figures

Grammar

1 Read these statements that were made by the interviewer or the interviewee during a job interview.

> We only recruit candidates from the best universities.

> You will spend a lot of your time meeting clients.

> Your starting salary will be around £30,000 per year.

> We are one of the biggest advertising agencies.
> Our clients include a number of private hospitals.

> You will be expected to attend in-service training.

> I can supply examples of my work as a copywriter.

> I really enjoy new challenges.

> We'll contact you before the end of the month.

2 Later, a colleague asks the candidate about the interview. Answer the colleague's questions by putting one of the above statements into reported speech. When you answer the questions which use *tell*, remember you also need to add the person after the verb.

1 What did they say about the salary?

   They said that my starting salary would be around £30,000
   per year.

2 What did they tell you about the company?

   ....

3 What did they say about training?

   ....

4 What did they tell you about the responsibilities of the job?

....

5 What did you tell them about your previous work?

....

6 What did they say about their recruitment policy?

....

7 What reason did you give for wanting the job?

....

8 When did they say they would be in touch?

....

Vocabulary

Some compound nouns refer to *types* of people. Complete the statements
(1–7) below, using the correct type of person from the box. Try to do this
without using a dictionary. Instead, look at the individual words which form
the compound nouns.

1 He finds it difficult to stop thinking about work and he's often in the office at
   weekends. He's a .workaholic.. .

2 I'm sure he'll move into a top position very soon because he's so ambitious.
   He's a real ....

3 She's never satisfied until a piece of work is as good as she can make it.
   She's a ....

4 He's definitely the best executive we've ever had and our market share has
   really improved under him. He's our ....

5 She's very good at working with other people and reducing conflict between
   them. She's a good ....

6 She tends to start rumours and she's annoyed several members of our team.
   I'm afraid she's a bit of a ....

7 He's very good at creative thinking and finding ways out of difficulties. He's a
   great ....

high flier perfectionist problem solver star performer
team player trouble maker ~~workaholic~~

Word list

Some of these words appear in the transcripts at the end of the Student's Book. U = unit, T = track, so U1 T1 means Unit 1 Track 1.

A

absentee *n* (p 105) a person who is not at work when they should be

absenteeism *n* (p 104) the problem of employees not being at work when they should be

access *n* (p 16) the opportunity to see or use something

accountant *n* (p 10) a person who keeps the records of money that is received and spent by a company

accounts *n* (p 11) the records of all the money that a company has received or spent

acquisition *n* (U18 T29) the purchase of one company by another

advertising campaign *n* (p 18) a series of activities to advertise something

agenda *n* (p 45) a list of things to be discussed in a meeting

agricultural *adj* (p 28) connected with farming

aisle *n* (p 46) the passage between seats in the middle of an aeroplane

anonymous *adj* (U23 T33) without the writer's name on it

applicant *n* (p 91) a person who applies for something, especially a job

appoint *v* (p 92) officially choose a person for a job

appraisal *n* (p 101) a meeting between an employee and their manager to discuss the employee's progress, aims and needs at work, or the report which summarises this meeting

appraisee *n* (U23 T33) the employee who is receiving the appraisal

appraiser *n* (p 101) the manager who gives the appraisal

approach *n* (p 56) a way of dealing with a situation or problem

assemble *v* (p 27) build something by joining different parts together

assembly *n* (p 79) the process of putting together parts (e.g. of a machine, product or structure)

asset *n* (p 86) something valuable belonging to a business (e.g. machinery) which could be used for the payment of debts

associate *n* (p 58) a person you know because of work or business

atmosphere *n* (p 11) the character or feeling of a place or situation

at the cutting edge (p 69) at the most recent stage of development

audiovisual equipment *n* (p 50) equipment that allows you to hear and see something (e.g. a presentation)

audit *n* (p 104) an official examination of something by an expert, usually the accounts of a business

authorise *v* (U6 T8) give official permission for something

autonomy *n* (p 56) a company's ability to choose and organise its own systems and activities

average *n* (p 67) a standard or level which is considered to be normal or the number obtained by adding two or more amounts together and dividing the total by the number of amounts

award *n* (p 18) a prize for achieving something

B

backfire *v* (p 23) have the opposite result from what you wanted

backlog *n* (U7 T10) a large amount of work or matters which are waiting to be done

balance sheet *n* (p 99) a document which shows a company's financial position, i.e. its wealth, assets and debts, at a particular time

ban *v* (p 57) not allow a person to do or have something

banker's card (also **bank card, cheque card**) *n* (p 35) a card which you show when you pay for something by cheque to show that the bank promises to pay

bankrupt *adj* (p 78) unable in law to pay debts and therefore forced to stop operating

banner *n* (p 39) an advertisement that appears across the top of a webpage

bar chart (also **bar graph**) *n* (p 74) a diagram in which different amounts are represented by rectangles of different length

be based in *v* (p 59) live or work mainly in this place

bear market *n* (p 83) a financial market where prices are falling

billboard *n* (p 18) a large board used to display advertisements outside

blade *n* (p 26) the sharp metal part of a machine or piece of equipment which is used to cut something

blend *v* (U6 T7) mix two or more things together

block booking *n* (p 67) a booking (e.g. for a hotel) for a group of people

boarding card (also **boarding pass**) *n* (p 46) the card that a passenger must have to show that they have passed security checks before getting on a plane

body language *n* (U14 T24) the movements and positions of your body which show other people how you are feeling, often without you knowing it

bond *n* (p 83) a certificate issued by a government or public company which promises to repay money at a fixed rate of interest at a specified time

bonus *n* (U14 T25) an extra amount of money paid to a person for good performance, or at a special time of the year

booked up *adj* (p 25) with no free places for extra appointments

bookkeeping *n* (p 10) the job of keeping a record of the money that is received and spent by a company

branch *n* (p 43) any of the offices or shops that belong to a large company

brand *n* (p 20) a type of product made by a company under a particular name

brand identity *n* (p 40) the values and qualities which people associate with a particular brand

break down barriers *v* (p 67) improve understanding and communication between people

break even *v* (p 78) have neither profit nor loss at the end of a business activity

break the ice *v* (p 67) make people who do not know each other well feel more relaxed with each other

break the news *v* (p 96) tell a person about something unpleasant which will affect or upset them

broadband *n* (p 22) a telecommunications system which allows information to be sent quickly between computers and other electronic equipment

broker *n* (p 82) a person who buys and sells shares for others

budget *n* (p 33) a plan which shows how much money you have and how you will spend it

budget holder *n* (p 33) the person responsible for a particular budget

building society *n* (p 85) a financial organisation that pays interest on members' savings and lends money for the purchase of property

bull market *n* (p 83) a financial market where prices are rising

business plan *n* (p 87) a document giving details of a company's expected sales, costs and future financial planning

C

cable *n* (p 26) a wire, usually covered by plastic, which carries electricity or telecommunication signals

call off *v* (U2 T3) decide not to do a planned activity (e.g. a meeting)

candidate *n* (p 91) a person who applies for a job

capacity *n* (p 51) the total amount that can be contained or produced

capital *n* (p 80) money used to invest, lend or borrow

capital employed *n* (p 80) the money that a business invests back into the company

card index *n* (p 26) a box for storing cards in a particular order

carrier *n* (p 40) a company, usually an airline, which transports goods or people from one place to another

cashflow *n* (p 81) the amount of money moving into and out of a business

catalogue *n* (U7 T10) a book with a list of all the goods you can buy from a shop or company

catering *n* (p 43) the activity of providing food and drink

chain *n* (p 20) a number of shops, hotels, etc. which are owned by the same company

chairman (also **chairwoman, chairperson**) *n* (p 56) the person in charge of a meeting, conference or organisation

challenge *n* (p 14) something that is difficult to do

challenging *adj* (p 15) difficult in a way which tests your ability or determination

channel *n* (p 39) a way of getting something done or a way of communicating with people

channel of distribution (also **distribution channel**) *n* (p 39) the way in which goods are transported from producers to buyers

charitable trust *n* (U3 T4) a trust which is formed with the aim of giving money to charity

chase payment *v* (p 78) try to make a person pay the money that they owe

check-in desk *n* (p 46) the place at the airport where you show your ticket, give in your luggage and receive your boarding card

classified ad *n* (p 39) a small advertisement in a newspaper or magazine

close a deal *v* (p 73) finalise a business agreement

cluttered *adj* (p 23) full of unnecessary things

colleague *n* (p 14) a person who you work with

collective *n* (p 20) a business which is owned or controlled by the people who work in it

come up with *v* (p 15) produce (an idea or suggestion)

commemorate *v* (U14 T25) officially remember, with respect, a person or an event, especially with a ceremony

commercial *n* (p 18) an advertisement on TV or radio

commission *n* (p 82) an amount of money paid to an agent for arranging a sale or purchase

committed *adj* (U15 T26) willing to give your time and energy to something that you believe in

commodity *n* (p 83) a substance or agricultural product that can be bought or sold in large amounts

compact *adj* (p 42) closely and neatly packed together to save space

competitive *adj* (p 15) equal to or better than others

competitor *n* (p 22) a person, company or product which is trying to be more successful than another in the same market

component *adj* (p 79) combining with other parts to form something bigger

compromise *n* (p 101) ending of an argument or difference of opinion by each side agreeing to some of the demands of the other

computer-literate *adj* (p 95) having knowledge of how to use and work with computers

conflict *n* (p 63) a serious disagreement or argument

connection *n* (p 42) a train or plane which passengers arriving on another train or plane can catch to continue their journey

consultancy *n* (p 61) a company that gives expert advice on a particular subject

consultant *n* (p 11) a person who advises people on a subject that he or she is an expert in

convert *v* (p 51) to change in form, character or use

cooperate *v* (p 66) work together for a particular purpose

cooperative *adj* (p 67) willing to work with people and do what they ask

coordinate *v* (p 11) make all the different people and different parts of an activity work together in an organised way

corporate rate *n* (p 100) a special price offered to companies

corporation *n* (p 89) a large company or group of companies which acts as a single organisation and is recognised as such in law

correspondence *n* (U1 T2) letters, especially official or business letters

counselling *n* (p 105) the process of listening to a person and giving them professional advice about their problems

courier *n* (p 37) a person who transports documents or products

courteous *adj* (p 72) polite and respectful

cover costs *v* (p 78) make enough money to pay for expenses

craftsman *n* (U5 T6) a person who uses special skills to make things, especially with their hands

crash *v* (p 29) suddenly stop working

crate *n* (p 59) a large box used for storing or moving things

creative *adj* (p 68) producing and using new and unusual ideas

credibility *n* (p 99) a person's ability to make other people believe and trust them

credit checking *n* (p 96) the activity of looking at a person's record of repaying loans and advising whether or not to give them a new loan

creditor *n* (p 78) a person or organisation that a company owes money to

crisis *n* (U15 T26) a situation which has reached a very difficult point, or a time of great disagreement and uncertainty

curriculum vitae *n* (p 90) a written description of a person's qualifications and previous employment

customs *pl n* (p 35) the place at an airport or port through which goods must pass to make sure they are not illegal and where any tax must be paid

cut off *v* (p 37) break the connection during a telephone call

D

data management *n* (p 88) control and organisation of information held on computer databases

deadline *n* (p 11) a time or day by which something must be done

deal *n* (p 73) a business agreement

debt *n* (p 48) money that is owed to a person or company

debtor *n* (p 78) a person or organisation that owes money to a company

decline *n* (p 18) a situation where something becomes less in number or amount

deficit *n* (p 81) the amount of money that a business has lost in a particular period of time

delegate *n* (p 51) a person sent to represent others at a conference

demanding *adj* (p 73) needing a lot of time, attention or energy

demonstrate *v* (p 43) show something (e.g. a product) and explain how it works

demonstration *n* (p 43) the act of showing something and explaining how it works

department store *n* (p 63) a large shop selling a variety of goods in different departments

departure lounge *n* (p 46) the area in an airport where passengers wait before they get on a plane

depression *n* (p 18) a long period when there is very little business activity and not many jobs

desalination *n* (p 72) the process of removing salt from sea water

device *n* (p 26) a piece of equipment which does a particular job

dip *n* (p 49) a movement downwards to a lower level or number

discount *n* (p 34) a reduction in the usual price

dismantle *v* (p 27) take something apart so that it is in several pieces

dismiss *v* (p 95) remove from a job, especially when a person has done something wrong

dissolve *v* (U6 T7) (of a solid) become part of a liquid

diverse *adj* (p 56) made up of a variety of different things or different types of people

dividend *n* (p 82) the part of a company's profits which is divided between its shareholders

dividend yield *n* (p 83) the amount of profit paid to shareholders, calculated as a percentage of the current share price

dominate *v* (U15 T26) have control over a person or group of people

downgrade *v* (p 52) reduce a person or thing to a lower position

download *v* (p 22) copy data from one computer system to another or to a disk

downturn *n* (p 84) a reduction in business activity

draw *n* (p 60) a competition where people are given numbered tickets which are chosen at random to decide winners of prizes

duty free shop *n* (p 46) a shop in an airport or on board a ship where you can buy goods without paying government tax

E

email overload *n* (p 103) a situation when you receive more emails than you can manage

engaged *adj* (p 44) (of a telephone line) unavailable because it's already being used by another person

entertain *v* (U14 T24) show hospitality to a business client (e.g. by taking them to an event or a restaurant)

entertainment *n* (p 42) action of showing hospitality

entrepreneur *n* (p 86) a person who starts up their own business, especially one which involves risk

equities *pl n* (p 83) stocks and shares which pay no fixed amount of interest

ethos *n* (p 60) the set of beliefs and ambitions which are typical of a group or company

etiquette *n* (p 73) the usual rules of polite behaviour in a certain social situation

evaporate *v* (p 31) (of a liquid) change into gas

evaporation *n* (p 31) the act of evaporating

exchange rate *n* (p 23) the amount of one currency which you can buy with a particular amount of another currency

executive *n* (p 11) a person in a high position in an organisation who makes decisions

exhibition *n* (p 18) an event where companies show their products to the public

expenditure *n* (p 78) the total amount of money that a person or business spends

expertise *n* (p 100) a high level of knowledge or skill

extend *v* (p 72) offer or give (e.g. your thanks to someone)

extension *n* (p 37) a telephone, especially one with its own additional number on a line leading from the main switchboard

extract *v* (p 31) take something out of something else

extraction *n* (p 31) the act of extracting something

eye-opener *n* (U23 T33) something that surprises you and teaches you new facts about people or life

F

face to face *adj* (U2 T3) looking directly at one another

fare *n* (p 40) the money a passenger must pay for a journey

fasten *v* (p 27) fix something together, or fix one thing to another

faulty *adj* (p 11) not well-made or not working correctly

fee *n* (p 49) payment in exchange for advice or services

feedback *n* (p 56) information about a product or person, used as a basis for improvement

file *n* (p 26) a type of container used to store documents

filing cabinet *n* (p 33) a piece of furniture in an office used for holding documents

financial year *n* (p 80) period of 12 months for which a company plans its financial management

fire *v* (p 95) see **dismiss**

flexible *adj* (p 15) able to be changed easily according to the situation

flipchart *n* (p 50) a board with large pieces of paper fixed at the top which can be turned over

float *v* (p 83) sell shares of a company on the stock market for the first time

flood *v* (p 89) arrive in large numbers

flotation *n* (p 83) the process of offering shares of a company for sale to the public for the first time

fluctuate *v* (p 75) rise and fall irregularly in number or amount

fluctuation *n* (p 75) an irregular rise and fall in number or amount

folder *n* (p 103) a collection of files kept together on a computer

follow-up *adj* (p 99) thing done or action taken to continue something done before

forecast *v* (p 39) say what you expect to happen in the future

format *n* (p 88) the way in which information is arranged and stored

forum *n* (p 69) a meeting for the exchange of opinions

founding *n* (p 18) start (a new company or organisation)

framework *n* (p 60) order or structure (e.g. of a meeting)

freight *n* (p 36) goods which are carried from one place to another by ship, rail, plane or truck

freight forwarding specialist *n* (p 36) a person or company who arranges for goods to be transported from one place to another

fulfilling *adj* (p 93) making you feel happy and satisfied

G

gadget *n* (p 26) a small piece of equipment which does a particular job

get down to *v* (p 73) begin to do or give serious attention to

get through *v* (p 37) succeed in speaking to somebody on the telephone

giant *n* (p 63) a very large, successful company

gimmick *n* (p 23) something which is used to get people's attention but which isn't very useful

glamour n (p 41) an attractive and exciting quality

glove compartment *n* (U10 T19) a small cupboard in the front of a car for storing small objects

goal *n* (p 105) an aim or purpose

graphic *n* (p 22) image which is shown on a computer screen

green *adj* (p 41) concerned with the protection of the environment

gross *adj* (p 78) total, before any costs or taxes are deducted

gross domestic product (GDP) *n* (p 76) the total value of goods and services which are produced within a country

gym (abbr. of **gymnasium**) *n* (p 50) a large room with equipment for doing physical exercises

H

hand in your notice *v* (p 95) tell your employer that you intend to leave your job

handling charge *n* (p 23) the cost of moving goods or money from one place to another

handout *n* (U15 T26) a piece of printed information, sometimes given by a speaker to their audience

hang up *v* (p 37) finish a telephone conversation and put the telephone down

hard copy *n* (p 24) a paper copy of information which came from a computer

harmony *n* (p 63) peacefulness or agreement

headquarters *pl n* (p 57) the managerial centre of an organisation

heavy duty *adj* (U7 T10) especially strong so that it can be used in difficult conditions

heavy goods train *n* (p 48) a train used for transporting large goods

hectic *adj* (U1 T1) very busy and fast

highlight *v* (p 91) attract attention to

high-tech *adj* (p 51) using the most advanced technology

hire *v* (p 95) employ a person to do a particular job

hold on *v* (p 37) wait for a short time

hold the line *v* (U7 T10) wait for a short time (on the telephone)

hole punch *n* (p 26) a small piece of equipment used for making holes in paper

home page *n* (p 22) the first page that you should see when you look at a website

hospitality *n* (p 40) the action of entertaining people in a welcoming and friendly way

host *n* (p 64) a person who invites other people as guests

human resources *pl n* (p 10) the part of a business that deals with finding new employees, keeping records of employees and helping them with any problems, etc.

I

icon *n* (p 103) a small picture or symbol on a computer screen which the user can click on with the mouse

IDD (International Direct Dialling) phone *n* (p 50) a phone which you can use to make international calls without going through an operator

implement *v* (p 69) put into action

impressed *adj* (p 72) feeling admiration for something

in due course *adv* (p 72) at a suitable time in the future

income statement *n* (p 99) a statement showing the amount of money earned and spent by a company in a particular period of time

inherit *v* (p 18) receive money or a business from a person after they have died

in-house *adj* (p 32) done within a company by its employees, not by people from outside the company

innovation *n* (p 41) the use of new ideas and methods

insolvency *n* (p 60) the situation when a company does not have enough money to pay its debts

intellectual property (IP) *n* (p 36) a person's or company's rights to profit from their idea or design (without another person copying it)

interact *v* (p 66) communicate and work together

interviewer *n* (p 94) the person who asks the candidate questions during an interview

in-tray *n* (p 69) a container on a desk for letters and documents to be dealt with later

invoice *n* (p 11) a list of things bought or work done with the price, for payment later

irrigation *adj* (p 72) dealing with supplying land with water so that plants can grow

J

jam *v* (p 29) become unable to work because a part is stuck

job security *n* (p 97) the situation of having a job which is likely to be permanent.

jobseeker *n* (p 91) a person who is looking for a job

L

label *n* (p 32) a small piece of paper, material, etc. attached to an object which gives information about it

laboratory *n* (p 11) a room or building with equipment for doing scientific tests

lapel pin *n* (p 60) a pin which is used to fasten something (e.g. a badge) to the front of your jacket

launch *v* (p 18) show a new product for the first time

laundry service *n* (p 53) a service offered by some hotels for washing, drying and ironing guests' clothes

lay off *v* (p 95) stop employing a worker temporarily or permanently because there is not enough work

lead *n* (p 26) a wire which connects a piece of electrical equipment to the electricity supply

leading *adj* (p 21) the most important

lecture *n* (p 51) a formal talk to a group of people on a particular subject

level off *v* (p 75) stop rising or falling and stay at the same level

lever *n* (p 26) a handle that you push or pull to make a machine work

life cycle *n* (p 39) the length of time that people continue to buy a particular product

lifespan *n* (p 38) the length of time a machine or piece of equipment is expected to last

line graph *n* (p 74) a diagram in which changes in amount over time are represented by a line

liquidation *n* (p 78) the situation when a company closes because of financial difficulties and its assets are sold to pay its debts

load *v* (p 22) abbreviation of **download**

loan *n* (p 86) the act of lending something, or the money which is lent

locker *n* (p 46) a small cupboard which can be locked, usually one of several placed together in a public place

log off *v* (p 35) stop a computer being connected to a computer system, when you want to finish working

logo *n* (p 23) a design or symbol which is used by a company to advertise its products

M

machinery *n* (p 72) a group of large machines or the parts of a machine which make it work

mailshot *n* (p 60) a piece of advertising material sent to a large number of addresses

maintenance *n* (p 69) the activity of keeping a building or machinery in good condition

make inroads *v* (U17 T28) start to have a noticeable effect

make someone redundant *v* (p 95) stop employing a person because there is no longer enough work for them, or because the company cannot afford to continue employing them

make up *v* (U17 T28) compose or form (part of something)

manic *adj* (U1 T1) very busy

marketing *n* (p 10) a group of activities to help sell a product or service by considering buyers' wants and needs

merge *v* (p 21) join together

merger *n* (p 88) the process when two or more companies join together to form a larger company

meticulous *adj* (U1 T1) very careful and paying a lot of attention to detail

mill *n* (p 20) a building fitted with machinery for a manufacturing process

minimal *adj* (p 62) of a very small amount

minutes *pl n* (U1 T2) the official record of what people say and decide during a meeting

mission *n* (p 60) the purpose or aim of an organisation

monitor *v* (p 88) watch and check for a period of time

motivation *n* (p 100) enthusiasm

motto *n* (p 60) a short sentence or phrase which expresses a belief or purpose

N

negotiate *v* (U12 T21) have formal discussions with a person in order to reach an agreement

net *adj* (p 78) remaining after deduction of tax and other costs

O

object *n* (p 67) the aim or purpose of doing something

offence *n* (U14 T24) feeling of annoyance or hurt

office politics *pl n* (p 56) the relationships (good and bad) between people who work in the same office

on the ball *adj* (p 101) showing up-to-date knowledge and/or an ability to think and act quickly

online *adj* (p 22) connected to the Internet

open-door management style *n* (p 16) a system where managers deal with employees' problems quickly and directly

operating profit *n* (p 78) the profit that a company makes from its usual activity

organiser *n* (p 42) a small file or diary where you record your appointments and other useful information

original *adj* (p 68) not the same as anything else and therefore special and interesting

outing *n* (p 73) a short trip taken for pleasure

outperform *v* (p 84) perform better than another

overheads *pl n* (p 78) the regular costs which are involved in running a business (e.g. rent or electricity)

overload *n* (p 103) too much of something

overspend *v* (p 78) spend more than was originally planned

overtake *v* (p 77) become a greater amount (than something else)

P

packaging *n* (p 21) the material put around goods before they are sold

packing list *n* (U7 T9) a list of goods that are packed and ready to send

panel *n* (p 56) a small group of people brought together to decide or discuss something

paper clip *n* (p 26) a small piece of bent metal used for holding papers together

participant *n* (p 67) a person who takes part or gets involved in something (e.g. a training course)

partition *n* (p 51) a structure, usually a thin wall, which separates one part of a room from another

patent *n* (p 36) the legal right to be the only person or company to make or sell an invention for a certain number of years

pay off *v* (p 78) pay back the full amount

payroll *n* (p 10) a list of people employed in a company, showing how much each person is paid

peak *n* (p 75) the highest point or value of something

pension *n* (p 16) money which is paid regularly to a person who has retired

pension fund *n* (U3 T4) an amount of money which people can pay into while working, which is then used to make regular payments to them after they retire

pension scheme *n* (p 16) a system into which an employee and employer make regular payments for a period of years, so that the employee can receive a pension when they retire

permanent *adj* (p 27) lasting for ever or for a very long time

personnel *pl n* (p 11) the people who work in an organisation

pharmaceutical *adj* (p 63) concerned with the preparation of medicinal drugs

philanthropist *n* (U3 T4) a person who gives money and help to people who need it

pick someone up *v* (U9 T14) collect a person or object from somewhere

pie chart *n* (p 74) a circle divided into parts that shows the way in which something (e.g. population or amount of money) is divided up

pliers *pl n* (p 27) a piece of equipment with two handles for pulling small things (e.g. nails) or for cutting wire

policy *n* (p 12) a set of rules or a plan of what to do in a particular situation

pool *v* (p 15) allow something to be collected and shared by everyone in a group

pop-up *n* (p 39) an advertisement which appears in a separate window on a webpage

portfolio *n* (p 84) a collection of investments; (p 92) all the products and services offered by a business

potential *n* (p 15) a person's or product's ability to develop and succeed

poverty *n* (U3 T4) the situation of being poor

premises *pl n* (p 28) the land and buildings owned by an organisation

pre-tax return *n* (p 80) the money that a company earns from something before tax is deducted

prioritise *v* (U1 T2) decide which tasks are the most important

privatise *v* (p 20) sell a company which is owned by the government to a private company or a member of the public

product positioning *n* (p 63) the way that people think about a product compared with competing products, or the way that the company would like them to think

production plant *n* (p 31) a place where an industrial or manufacturing process takes place

productivity *n* (p 32) a measure which compares the value of what a company produces with the time and money which it spends producing it

profile *n* (p 91) a short description of a person (or company) which gives only the most important details

profitability *n* (U18 T29) the state of producing a profit

promote *v* (p 32) encourage the popularity and sales of a product

promotion *n* (p 94) the situation when a person is raised to a higher or more important position in their work

proposal *n* (p 15) a suggestion, sometimes a written one

public relations (PR) *pl n* (p 39) the activity of keeping good relationships between an organisation and the public

pull funding *v* (p 96) stop giving money for something

pump money into *v* (p 88) spend a lot of money on something to try to make it successful

punctual *adj* (p 65) arriving or doing things at the correct time, not later

purchase *v* (p 24) buy

put down to *v* (p 61) think something is caused by something else in particular

put forward *v* (p 15) state (an opinion or suggestion) for other people to consider

put off *v* (p 47) arrange to delay an event or appointment until a later time

put through *v* (p 37) connect a person to another telephone extension

Q

quality control *n* (p 11) the activity of looking at goods or services to make sure that they are of the correct standard

questionnaire *n* (U12 T22) a list of questions, usually with a choice of answers, in order to collect information about a subject

quit *v* (p 95) leave (e.g. a job)

R

racecourse *n* (p 85) a ground or track for horse or dog racing

raise money *v* (p 87) collect money

recover *v* (p 75) improve after a period of weakness or low value

recovery *n* (p 75) the process of improving after a period of weakness or low value

recruitment *n* (p 92) the process of finding new people to work for a company

recruitment agency *n* (p 92) a business that makes its money by finding suitable people for employers who need new workers

redundant *adj* (p 95) no longer employed because there is not enough work

referee *n* (p 90) a person who confirms in writing an applicant's character or ability

reference *n* (p 91) a letter from a previous employer or teacher to confirm a person's ability or reliability

referral *n* (p 60) the act of directing someone to another person or place for help or business

refresher course *n* (p 98) a training course to bring a person's knowledge up to date, especially knowledge needed for a job

relocation *n* (p 88) the process of moving to a new place

rep *n* (p 43) (abbr. of **representative**)

representative *n* (p 43) an agent of a company who travels to clients to sell products

reschedule *v* (p 46) change the arranged time of something

research and development (**R and D**) *n* (p 10) the department in a business which deals with planning new products and trying to improve existing ones

resign *v* (p 108) leave a job because you want to

résumé *n* (US) (p 90) see **curriculum vitae**

retailer *n* (p 11) a person who sells products to the public

retire *v* (p 44) stop working because of old age or ill health

return *n* (U18 T29) a profit from an investment

revenue *n* (p 78) an organisation's income or the money it receives

review *n* (p 69) check in order to decide if changes should be made

revolutionise *v* (p 99) completely change something so that it is much better

rewarding *adj* (p 15) satisfying because you feel it is important or useful

ring off *v* (p 37) finish a telephone conversation and put the telephone down

rivet *n* (p 18) a small round piece of metal on a pair of jeans; (p 27) a metal pin, usually used to join pieces of metal together

road tax *n* (U10 T18) a tax you must pay on your vehicle before you are allowed to drive it on the road

role *n* (p 15) the position or purpose that a person has in an organisation

rumour *n* (p 56) an interesting story, which may or may not be true, that people are talking about

run out *v* (p 29) be used up so that there is none left

S

sack *v* (p 50) see **dismiss**

safe *n* (p 50) a locked cupboard where you can keep money and other valuable items

sales channel *n* (p 35) the way or place in which something is sold

sample *n* (p 32) an example product

savings *pl n* (U20 T31) money kept in a bank to use later

search engine *n* (p 22) a computer program which finds information on the Internet using words that you type in

sector *n* (p 84) a distinct part of the economy

secure a loan *v* (p 86) make certain that money which is lent will be paid back by giving the lender the right to own an asset (e.g. the house) of the borrower, if the money is not paid back

sell off *v* (p 96) get rid of something by selling it cheaply

seminar *n* (p 29) a meeting of a group of people for discussion or training

set up *v* (p 24) organise (e.g. an event); (p 18) start (a new business)

share *n* (p 20) any of the equal parts into which a company's capital is divided

shareholder *n* (p 82) a person who owns shares in a company

shelf-life *n* (p 108) the length of time that a product, especially food, can be kept in a shop before it becomes too old to sell

shortlist *v* (p 92) put a person on a list of candidates from which a final choice is made

shredder *n* (p 26) a machine used to destroy documents by cutting them into very small pieces

shuttle *n* (p 48) a vehicle or aeroplane that travels regularly between two places

sick leave *n* (p 104) the length of time that an employee is allowed to be absent from work because of illness and still receive pay

sick pay *n* (p 105) the money that an employer pays to a person who is absent from work because of illness

slogan *n* (p 21) a short phrase used in advertising which is easy to remember

small ad *n* (p 39) see **classified ad**

small talk *n* (p 65) polite conversation about unimportant things

soar *v* (p 49) rise quickly to a high level or number

spectrum *n* (U14 T24) the range of possible opinions, feelings or ways of behaving

spreadsheet *n* (p 104) a computer program for doing financial calculations and plans

springboard *n* (U1 T1) something which puts someone in a good position to start a process or career

staffing *n* (p 61) the action of providing employees for an organisation

stake *n* (p 83) a share or interest in a company

stalemate *n* (p 101) a situation where neither side in an argument can win and no action can be taken

stand *n* (U12 T22) a temporary display area where products are shown, often at a conference or trade fair

stand for *v* (p 66) be an abbreviation of or symbol for

standard *adj* (p 14) usual or normal

stapler *n* (p 26) a small piece of equipment used to fix papers together by pushing a small piece of metal through them

state-of-the-art *adj* (p 51) using the most recent technology and ideas

static *adj* (p 77) staying at the same value without changing for a long period of time

stationery *n* (U6 T8) things which you use for writing (e.g. pens and paper)

stereotype *n* (U20 T32) a fixed idea, especially one that is wrong, that people have about a type of person or thing

stock exchange *n* (p 82) the place where stocks and shares in companies are bought and sold

stock *v* (p 11) provide something for people to buy

stock *n* (p 82) shares, or a certain number of shares

strategy *n* (p 14) a plan for achieving success

stylish *adj* (p 42) of high quality in appearance and design

suite *n* (p 52) a set of connected rooms in a hotel

supplier *n* (p 32) a company which provides products or services

survey *n* (p 55) a study of the opinions of a group of people, based on a list of questions

surveyor *n* (U20 T32) a person who measures and records the details of areas of land or a person who is trained to examine buildings and discover if there are any problems with the structure

switchboard *n* (p 37) a piece of equipment for the manual control of telephone connections

T

take over *v* (p 18) get control of or responsibility for something (e.g. a company)

talented *adj* (U15 T26) having a natural ability to be good at something

tap into *v* (p 88) make use of something, especially people's interest or ability

target *n* (p 32) a result that you intend to achieve

target market *n* (p 32) the group of people that a product is aimed at

task *n* (p 56) a piece of work

team-building *n* (p 56) encouraging people to build relationships with each other and work together as a team

telemarketing *n* (p 60) selling goods or services by telephone

temporary *adj* (p 27) lasting for only a short time

thriving *adj* (p 49) growing and successful

time-consuming *adj* (p 23) needing a lot of time

to the point *adj* (p 65) directly expressed and suitable for the topic being discussed

tool *n* (p 27) a piece of equipment which you use with your hands to make or repair something

trade fair *n* (p 36) an event where companies show and sell their products to retailers or other companies who work in the same field

trademark *n* (p 36) a legally registered name or symbol which represents a company or product and cannot be used by another company

trainee *n* (p 98) a person who is being taught certain skills for a job

trend *n* (p 74) a general direction in which something is developing or changing

trust *n* (U3 T4) an organisation which controls money or property for the benefit of other people

turn down *v* (p 92) reject or refuse

turnover *n* (p 61) the amount of business done in a particular period, measured by the value of the goods or services sold

U

unemployment rate *n* (p 76) the percentage of the working population who do not have a job

unwrap *v* (p 64) remove the paper or material that covers something

up to date *adj* (p 23) modern or containing the most recent information

update *v* (p 22) make something more modern or give the most recent information to someone

upgrade *v* (p 28) improve the quality or usefulness of something

V

vacancy *n* (p 93) a job that no one is doing (and therefore available for a new person to do)

vat *n* (p 31) a large container for mixing or storing liquids, especially in a factory

venture *n* (p 89) a new business activity which involves risk or uncertainty

venture capitalist *n* (p 108) a person who makes money available for investment in a new company, especially a risky one

venue *n* (p 48) the place where an event or meeting takes place

videoconferencing *n* (p 50) a telecommunications system in which two or more people in different parts of the world can talk to each other and see each other on a TV screen

voicemail *n* (p 42) an electronic telephone answering system

voluntary *adj* (p 92) done willingly, without being paid for it

voting buttons *n* (p 103) an email system where a group of people are asked the same question which they answer by clicking a button with their chosen reply

W

warehouse *n* (p 37) a large building for storing goods before they are sold

welfare *n* (p 10) a person's health and happiness

wind up *v* (p 60) gradually bring an activity to an end

wisdom *n* (p 69) the ability to use your knowledge and experience to make good judgements

word of mouth *n* (p 39) the process of getting to know about a product by hearing about it from friends, colleagues, etc.

workforce *n* (p 17) the group of people who work in a company

wrap *v* (p 64) cover something with paper or material

wrapper *n* (p 21) a piece of paper or plastic which covers something that you buy (especially food)

write off a debt *v* (p 78) cancel the record of a debt that will not be paid

Answer key

Unit 1
Vocabulary
1 **Personnel:** staff, recruitment, workforce, human resources
   Accounts: payroll, salary, bookkeeping, expenditure
   Sales: retail outlet, consumer, mail order, wholesale
3 1 product   2 producer
   3 production   4 productivity
4 Suggested words
   employee, employer, employment, employed, unemployed

Grammar
Suggested answers
2 What do people like on Marie Riley's show?
3 Is David Webb worried by the figures?
4 Who is Radio Heartbeat trying to appeal to?
5 Why is David Webb sure that Johnny can bring listeners in?/ Why does David Webb have confidence in Johnny?
6 What is Morgan Wells thinking of doing?

Unit 2
Reading
after-work activities   5
working hours   4
equal opportunities   2

Vocabulary
1 Suggested answers

verb–noun	adjective–noun
take responsibility	strong commitment
commission a report	professional qualifications
encourage movement	flexible working
provide support	intensive work
	keen sportsperson

2 1b   2d   3c   4a
3 Suggested answers
   credit card; credit facility; current account; current rate; deposit account; standing order; overdraft rate; overdraft facility; direct debit; cash account; cash card; cash point; cash dispenser; interest rate; mortgage rate
4 2 deposit account
   3 interest rate
   4 standing order
   5 direct debit

Unit 3
Grammar
2 2 ran   3 did not make   4 limited
   5 did not operate   6 did not have
3 Suggested answers
   2 What did the company manufacture at first?
   3 Where did Azim Premji study?
   4 When did Azim Premji take over the company? When did Mr M.H. Premji die?
   5 In the 70s and 80s, why did many multinational companies stop trading in India/leave India?
   6 When did Azim Premji set up the first IT business in Bangalore?

Writing

2 Sample answer

Rachel Elnaugh was born in Chelmsford, UK in 1965. She left school in 1983 and went to work in an accountant's office. In 1985 she moved to London where she worked as a tax consultant. In 1989, she first had the idea for the company 'Red Letter Days'. The idea came from trying to find a special birthday present for her father. In 1991, she started advertising the company in the national newspapers. In 2000, 'Red Letter Days' opened their branch in Scotland and in 2004, they opened their third office. In 2005, AIC took over the management of the company.

Unit 4

Writing

3 Sample answer

Dear Adam

Thanks for the excellent presentation. We should definitely do it again as soon as we can for those people who missed it. Can you suggest a time?

We just need to wait until your team have finished the trial period and then we're ready to start the new system.

Best wishes

Jo

Vocabulary

1 2 a 3 g 4 f 5 i 6 h 7 e 8 c 9 b

2 2 virus 3 screensaver 4 hackers 5 spam 6 server

Unit 5

Vocabulary

1

Noun	Adjective
a circle	circular
an oval	oval
a triangle	triangular
a square	square
a sphere	spherical
a cylinder	cylindrical
a cone	conical

2 a V-shaped b pear-shaped c star-shaped d mushroom-shaped

3 2 a 3 g 4 e 5 f 6 c 7 d 8 h

5 2 A 3 B 4 B 5 B 6 A 7 A

6 2 The toner in the photocopier needs changing.
3 The photocopier keeps overheating.
4 The computer keyboard needs cleaning.
5 The buttons on the machine keep jamming.

Unit 6

Grammar 1

2 The bathrooms are inspected every three hours.
3 Previous invoices are kept in the filing cabinet.
4 The staff are paid on the last working day of the month.
5 Discounts are given for all orders over £300.
6 All the bags are checked by the security guard.
7 Gloves are worn when mixing the oil.
8 The perfume bottles are packed into boxes by machines.
9 Cold air is blown over the mixture to cool it.

Vocabulary

2 dissolves 3 evaporates 4 distil
5 extract

Grammar 2

2 2 is distilled 3 is used 4 does
not go 5 are dried 6 are used
7 includes 8 are sold
9 are exported 10 employ
11 are taken on 12 remains
13 work

Unit 7

Grammar

1 2 should not 3 don't have to
4 must not 5 should not
6 can must should not

2 2 must not/can't 3 should
4 don't have to/shouldn't
5 must/have to 6 can't/mustn't

Vocabulary

1 The following answers are
possible:
2 A and B 3 B and C 4 A and C
5 A (British English) and
B (US English) 6 A and C
7 A and C 8 A and B

2 Suggested answer
A Baron Electronics. How can I help?
B I'd like to speak to Mr Rosen,
please.
A He's not here at the moment. Can I
take a message?
B Yes. Please could you ask him to
phone me as soon as possible?
A Can I ask you who's calling
please?
B Yes. It's Mr Reinhardt from the
Cooperative Bank.
A How do you spell your name?
B R-E-I-N-H-A-R-D-T

Unit 8

Vocabulary

Across: 4 logo 6 banner
7 competitor 11 market share
12 flyer
Down: 1 slogan 2 commercial
3 billboard 5 market leader
8 campaign 9 word of mouth
10 agency

Grammar

1 2 a 3 e 4 d 5 f 6 b

2 2 because many people are
annoyed by uninvited phone
calls.
3 so it is important to carry out
market research.
4 so companies have to
continually develop new ones.
5 so they often continue to buy a
particular one.
6 because people tell their friends
about both good and bad
experiences.

3 2 in order to 3 in order to 4 so
5 Because 6 so

Unit 9

Grammar

2 'm flying 3 'm coming
4 'm staying 5 are you going to do
6 'm going to check 7 will fall

Vocabulary

1 2 made 3 is going to make
4 make 5 makes 6 made
7 made 8 to do/do 9 is doing

Unit 10

Vocabulary 1

1 2 boarding card/pass 3 aisle seat
4 flight attendant, board/get on the
plane/flight 5 swap seats
6 emergency exit, overhead locker
7 get off the plane

2 Suggested answers
2 b   3 a   4 f   5 e   6 d   7 h   8 c

3 Suggested answers
You check in your bags.
You receive a boarding card.
You show your passport and
boarding card.
You go through the security check.
You board the plane.
You put your hand luggage in the
locker.
You fasten your seat belt.
The plane takes off.

Grammar
2 Although   3 However   4 Despite

Vocabulary 2
Suggested answers
1 **prospered**: become richer
2 **exceeded**: was more than
3 **plunged**: fallen
  withstood: survived

Unit 11
Vocabulary
1 2 not far from   3 before
4 reservation   5 obtain (insurance)
6 extend   7 recommend   8 leave

Writing
1 2 B   3 A   4 A   5 B   6 A   7 A
2 Sample answer
Thank you for your email of 3
June regarding booking an
apartment. I attach details of
suitable apartments which are
available on the dates you require.
Although we do not run a cleaning
service, we can provide contact
details of local cleaning agencies. I
would advise you to book as soon
as possible as demand is high.

Unit 12
Grammar
Suggested answers
3 the most useful   4 larger
5 the dullest   6 longer   7 more
helpful   8 more entertaining

Vocabulary
1 Suggested answers
wear a badge; give a lecture/a
presentation; put up signs; attend a
presentation/a lecture; book the
venue; give out a feedback
form/information packs; fill in a
feedback form

2
a delegate: attend a lecture/a
presentation; fill in a feedback
form
a speaker: give a presentation/
lecture
an organiser: book the venue; give
out information packs/a feedback
form; put up signs
all three: wear a badge

Unit 13
Grammar
2 chose   3 earned   4 became
5 has been   6 has expanded   7 has
become   8 has established   9 passed
10 has always insisted   11 have called
12 have made

Reading
2 e   3 g   4 d   5 f   6 c   7 a

Vocabulary
Suggested answers
take the opportunity, build up
contacts, etc.

Unit 14

Grammar

2 d   3 b   4 e   5 h   6 f   7 i   8 a
9 g

Vocabulary

1

Adjective	Opposite
lucky	unlucky
fortunate	unfortunate
successful	unsuccessful
formal	informal
polite	impolite
friendly	unfriendly
patient	impatient
comfortable	uncomfortable
clear	unclear
popular	unpopular
common	uncommon
likely	unlikely
usual	unusual
official	unofficial

2   1 unsuccessful   2 unofficial
3 unpopular

Unit 15

Vocabulary

1

Verb	Noun
organise	organisation
arrange	arrangement
communicate	communication
appreciate	appreciation
equip	equipment

2

Verb	Noun	Adjective
entertain	entertainment	entertaining
excite	excitement	exciting
attract	attraction	attractive
enjoy	enjoyment	enjoyable
protect	protection	protective
benefit	benefit	beneficial

3   2 enjoyable   3 attractive
4 exciting   5 appreciation

Writing

1   Spelling mistakes: interested,
corporate, grateful, available,
please, whether, travel, sincerely
2   2 a   3 d   4 e   5 b
Sample answer

Thank you for your email
enquiring about our chocolate
workshops.

Group workshops can take place
either at our venue or at yours.

I attach a list of possible dates
and times.

We are always willing to try to
arrange alternative dates.

Please do not hesitate to contact
me on 0208 746583 if none of
the attached dates are suitable.

Unit 16

Grammar

1

Countable	Uncountable
increase	revenue
grinder	coffee
machine	food
profit	bread
	equipment
	feedback
	evidence
	research
	room

2   The correct sentences are:
2 We really need to get some
feedback from our customers.
3 There is not much evidence to
suggest that our clientele is
getting younger.
4 We are going to replace all of
this equipment.

5 All of <u>this information needs</u> to be entered into the computer.

Writing

Sample answers

A

Dear Mr Kitson

I am writing to thank you for your very entertaining lecture at the conference last week. The feedback that we received about the event was almost entirely positive and a large number of delegates said that your lecture was the most interesting of the conference. Thank you again for helping to make the event a success.

Yours sincerely

Jonathon Gabriel

B

Dear Robert

Thanks very much for the wonderful meal last night. It was lovely to meet Barbara and please pass on our thanks to her as well.

From

Tony and Sarah

Unit 17

Grammar

2 Sample answer

In 1990, the unemployment rate stood at just over 2 per cent. *It rose slightly* over the next three years and then in 1993, *there was a sharp increase* to over 4 per cent. During the next two years *there was a slight fall*, but then it increased again to reach over 6 per cent at the beginning of 1999. After that, *it dipped again*, but then *there was a dramatic rise*. The rate hit 8 per cent in 2001. *It rose more gradually* over the following three years.

3 2 steady 3 strongly 4 recent
5 sharply 6 completely
7 unexpected 8 confident

Vocabulary

Company X

1 The share price rose slightly on Monday and continued …
2 … to climb the following day. However, …
3 … Wednesday saw an end to this upward trend as the price levelled off.
4 There were no further increases on Thursday either but unfortunately on Friday …
5 … the price suddenly plunged to just below Monday's value.

Company Y

1 The share price showed a slight fall on Monday and continued …
2 … to go down the following day. However, …
3 Wednesday saw an end to this downward trend as the price stabilised.
4 There were no further drops in price on Thursday either but on Friday there was a complete change of fortune as …
5 … the price suddenly recovered and rose sharply to exceed even Monday's value.

Unit 18

Vocabulary

1 2 5,940   3 750   4 810   5 7,540
   6 6,100   7 840   8 1,000

2 1 total overheads   2 gross profit

3
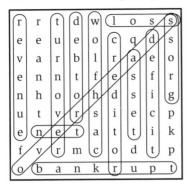

1 creditor   2 debtor   3 turnover
4 revenue   5 overheads   6 loss
7 bankrupt   8 gross   9 net
10 deficit   11 cashflow   12 asset

Unit 19

Grammar

1

Cause	Effect
In December people often feel positive about the New Year	They buy more in winter
People are on holiday in July and August	People buy less in the summer
The stock market is influenced by many different things	It is difficult to predict
Big gains in share prices usually happen very suddenly	They are over before investors can take advantage of them

2 2 because
   3 so
   4 However
   5 because
   6 so

Vocabulary

Across: 6 portfolio   8 bull
9 subsidiary   10 stake   11 flotation
12 merger   13 dividend
Down: 1 capital   2 returns   3 stock
4 commodities   5 broker   7 bonds
8 bear

Unit 20

Grammar

1 2 which   3 who   4 which
   5 which   6 who   7 which

2 2 playing board games
   3 moral or religious board games
   4 $50   5 'Banking'   6 $100
   7 George S. Parker Company
   8 the board games industry
   9 Monopoly   10 Charles Darrow
   11 Charles Darrow

Vocabulary

1 2 poured   3 took out   4 flood
   5 back up   6 raise   7 invested
   8 cutting

Unit 21
Vocabulary
1

Adjective	Noun
punctual	punctuality
polite	politeness
rude	rudeness
generous	generosity
kind	kindness
sincere	sincerity
original	originality
courteous	courtesy
reliable	reliability
creative	creativity
sensitive	sensitivity
loyal	loyalty

2 2 original   creativity
3 helpfulness   courtesy
4 loyal   stability   5 sensitivity
3 2 g   3 a   4 f   5 d   6 b   7 h   8 c
4

Adjective	Noun
precise	precision
accurate	accuracy
certain	certainty

Unit 22
Grammar
1 2 e   3 d   4 a   5 b   6 f
2 2 would   3 would   4 will   5 will

Vocabulary
2 graduated
3 curriculum vitae
4 turned down
5 human resources
6 lay off
7 redundant
8 redundancy
9 graduate
10 curriculum vitae
11 newspaper ads

Unit 23
Vocabulary

```
p a m m c w z m l p n y p
g p s x r h r e f e r e e
s p r v l f o i f r c e q
h r é j w l i z z s b l o
o a s j t o w k o o p c n
r i u s u g g f t n y n u
t s m q i p y y o n t o a
l a é l a y o f f e d t p
i l k c j d t j g l o i v
s f l p r o m o t e p c h
t w o r k f o r c e b e b
d i s m i s s v h b p j o
y a u j y x r e t i r e r
d q w t u r n d o w n n c
```

1 résumé   2 promote   3 lay off
4 workforce   5 shortlist   6 dismiss
7 referee   8 notice   9 appraisal
10 turn down   11 retire
12 personnel

Grammar
2 performance   3 management
4 interruptions   5 seriously
6 knowledge   7 criticism(s)
8 demotivated   9 improve
10 avoid   11 measure   12 promptly

Unit 24
Grammar
2 2 They told me (that) they were
one of the biggest advertising
agencies and (that) their clients
included a number of private
hospitals.
3 They said (that) I would be
expected to attend in-service
training.

4 They told me (that) I would spend a lot of my time meeting clients.
5 I told them (that) I could supply examples of my work as a copywriter.
6 They said (that) they only recruited candidates from the best universities.
7 I said (that) I really enjoyed new challenges.
8 They said (that) they would contact me before the end of the month.

Vocabulary
2 high flier
3 perfectionist
4 star performer
5 team player
6 trouble maker
7 problem solver

Notes